MY FATHER'S SON

Bridging Generations:
The Courageous Journey of
My Father and Grandfather

A MEMOIR

JOE AMRA

For more information, visit jamra.eas@gmail.com
ISBN: 979-8-9929222-0-2 (hardcover)
ISBN: 979-8-9929222-1-9 (paperback)
ISBN: 979-8-9929222-2-6 (eBook)

Library of Congress Control Number: 2025907062

Cover and Interior Design by Kelly Nielsen, Studio 92

This book is based on true events, many of which were related to the author by his father. It also reflects the author's present recollections of experiences over time. This book represents the personal views and opinions of the author and does not necessarily reflect the positions or opinions of any individual with which the author is affiliated. The content presented herein is based on the author's perspective and interpretation of the subject matter. Neither the author nor any associated parties shall be held responsible for any consequences arising from the opinions or interpretations expressed within this book.

Dedication

I dedicate this memoir to my wife, Insaf, my five children, my grandchildren, and all future generations of my family.

Table of Contents

Preface vii

Meet the Amra Family xi

1   A Paper-Folded Passport 1

2   The Journey Continues 9

3   Way of Life 29

4   Police Force Adventures 33

5   Traveling to Venezuela 43

6   Grandfather's Stay 57

7   New Beginnings 65

8   Back to Venezuela 75

9   Return to Palestine 79

10 Transitioning to America 93

11 Falls Church 105

12 Time in Tennessee 119

Epilogue: Words of Wisdom 133

Memory Lane 145

About the Author 147

Connect with Joe Amra 149

Preface

Growing up, listening to my father share stories and adventures about his life and my grandfather's was always fascinating to me. Though they have passed, I couldn't think of a better way to honor them both and preserve their legacy. That is what this book is all about; the lessons I have learned from them are invaluable and something I want to pass along to my family now and for generations to come.

Even though I was only four when we left Palestine and vaguely remember my grandfather, when I look back on his life, I often think about what his life was like and what drove him to leave his country and travel to the other side of the world. Most Palestinians would leave for a place where they could find work. In his case, he made the decision to board a passenger ship for a thirty-day journey to South America in 1924. After all, there were no airplanes to board in those days.

I often wonder what prompted him to do that, other than looking for prosperity and a way to make a living for his family. What did he or anyone in the area where he lived know about the sea? There had to be some anxiety over that decision, but there was no other option, not to mention knowing that he would be so far from home.

If I could make one wish today, I would spend five minutes with him to understand his thought process. I would ask him about all the adventures of building an entirely new life over twenty-seven years, before he went back to Palestine. It was like he lived three different lives—one up to the age of twenty-four, when he left his wife and son, then living another new life with a whole new family for many years.

After establishing a new successful life of prosperity, he reached out to find out if family members in Palestine still existed. When he made contact, he discouraged his son—my father—from coming to see him, because he didn't want my father to know he had started a new life.

Stubborn beyond belief, it was like pulling teeth to get him to revisit his prior life, but, as you will learn, he finally decided to do so, and realized how much he missed his first wife and his life in Palestine. His life was a culmination of three significant periods of time.

Thinking about my father's journey in life and what he experienced, I can't imagine having to grow up without a father, living under the abusive rule of an uncle, with my grandmother in poverty mode during his childhood.

Then, an opportunity presented itself that would go against everyone's wishes: He was recruited to become a policeman under the British command, something that Palestinians were resisting at the time, since the British occupied Palestine. However, he considered it a way to protect his family, earn a significant income, and protect other Palestinians.

Then, at twenty-two, out of the blue, he received a communication from his father, who had left him behind. I can't imagine what that must have felt like, or what went through his mind, heart, and soul. His father—my grandfather—had left him when he was a year old, but at that point, he was probably thinking he didn't want to live without knowing the challenges my grandfather had faced in his life.

However, a voice inside told him, This is your father, and wouldn't it be great to have an opportunity to meet this person? Whether you go there or he came to see you?

No doubt, he couldn't help but be curious about the father he didn't know. I wish I had thought about this situation more and discussed it with my father when he was alive, along with so many other things that I have thought about since his passing.

Like his father, my father also lived three lives: first as a child of poverty, then as a successful policeman, and then when his father returned to his life. There are all sorts of twists and turns to the story about when he traveled to South America to meet him. He had all kinds of issues when he returned to Palestine, from discovering an odd development with his first wife to becoming involved with politicians in the Jordanian government.

During the outbreak of war in 1967, he had to consider the safety and prosperity of his family, and, ultimately, moved to America. This decision was significant because it meant uprooting his entire family and relocating to another country.

Starting a new life in the United States was both thrilling and stressful. My father's journey, sacrifices, and desire to provide us with a better life are why I had to tell this story—to honor my grandfather's accomplishments and aspirations. I can see traces of my father and grandfather in our children, from their stubbornness to their mannerisms.

We constantly talk about them, and as our children learn more about their ancestors' experiences, it brings them closer to us and awakens their memory. I can't imagine not writing this book for us and for them. What a wonderful gift. I hope you enjoy the ride.

Meet the Amra Family

From left to right: Insaf, Sharin, Shahira, Sharuk, Sharihan, Jamil, and Joe.

We are thrilled to share the stories and adventures of my grandfather and great-grandfather. All of us, including our mother, Insaf, wanted to share our thoughts about having our family history documented in this book. As you can imagine, getting all of us together for a meeting to share our reflections was a challenge, but thank goodness for the modern technology of Zoom.

Insaf

I have always talked about my in-laws fondly, as we all lived in the same house when Joe and I first married. My mother-in-law was like a second mother to me; we had a very loving relationship. My daughters and I were very close to my in-laws, and we spent a lot of time together. They didn't want to live anywhere else, so our daughters had a close relationship with their grandparents.

Reading through this book is like traveling back in time, but it feels like the present as the adventures of my father-in-law and his father unfold. I remember when my father-in-law walked into a room, everyone knew it. He stood tall with a strong presence, and when he spoke, everyone

Joe and Insaf

listened because he always had such interesting stories to share. Many people respected him, especially because of the way he presented himself, always dressed in a nice suit and tie, ready for the day. Every morning, he would wake up around 7:30 am, take a bath, shave, and get dressed before having his coffee.

My husband, Joe, admits that he was his role model and is very much like his father and grandfather in many ways. We are grateful that our children feel proud of us, and are glad that we raised them to be strong and independent people. It runs in the family, and we all hope you enjoy reading about their adventures.

Sharihan

As the oldest child, I have the most vivid memories of sitting with my grandfather as he told me stories about everything and anything. But the story of him and my great-grandfather was one I wanted to hear over and over again. Maybe it was the way he told the story, the story itself, or maybe both, and I never took those warm memories for granted whenever I had the opportunity to listen to him.

My grandfather always held his head high and displayed a tough exterior, but despite overcoming many obstacles in his lifetime, his heart was gold for those he loved and cherished in his life. This book is an heirloom that will never die. It has been written for all of us, our children, and their children, generation after generation. This book is a way to keep my grandfather's spirit alive. We can all agree that my dad is who he is today because of his upbringing and that of

From left to right: Tayer, daughters Innaya and Ayla, son, Nayef, and Sharihan

my grandfather and great-grandfather.

I often recall my father talking about writing a book, even brainstorming potential titles. Now that he has accomplished his goal, it has enriched everyone involved. It is lovely to have a piece of our family's history documented in a book that we can share with others and our children, who never will have the pleasure of knowing my grandfather and great-grandfather.

It is important to know my grandfather's and his father's experiences from my dad's perspective. I am so proud of the upbringing I have been blessed with and am forever thankful to my dad for keeping this history alive by allowing others to read about it and hopefully be immersed in this remarkable story. I hope those who read the book will be able to relate to my grandfather's and great-grandfather's life events and experiences.

Sharin

My dad has always spoken with immense pride about our family and ancestors, especially when recounting stories about his father and grandfather. As I was growing up, I always felt that same pride whenever he shared stories of their lives. As I've listened to these stories over my lifetime and learned about the challenges they faced and the difficult journeys they took, I have come to understand how their unwavering resilience shaped my dad into the person he is today.

He embodies determination and humility; qualities he has always encouraged us to reflect in our lives. I've been deeply privileged to witness the profound respect people always showed my grandfather when they were in his presence, and it fills me with immense pride to see that same respect now being shown to my dad.

Yazeed and Sharin with daughter Ameelia

I am incredibly proud of the strong foundation my father, grandfather, and great-grandfather have built for our family—one that spans past, present, and future generations. I believe readers will feel the same connection when they read about their incredible life experiences. It is an honor to have our family's history preserved in this book, and I hope it ensures that our culture, values, and legacy continue to be cherished for generations to come.

Sharuk

As a young attorney, I learned early on that hard work and determination run in the family, as you will learn in this book. I have heard many of these stories growing up, but never in their entirety, so I am grateful for my dad sharing the progression of what my grandfather and great-grandfather went through in more detail.

All of us can pass this on to our children and grandchildren. There is something timeless about putting words to paper and into a book. In general, telling stories can be like playing telephone, and things can get lost in translation, or some details may unintentionally be left out. That is why I appreciate that these are stories from my dad's perspective. I see this book as a special treasure we will have forever.

Though a prosecutor, I hope to handle the copyright when it's time to turn this book into a movie.

Shahira

As the youngest daughter in our family, I agree with my older sisters and want to add that this book mirrors everything I heard about while growing up. I have the best memories of my dad telling us stories about my grandfather. Whether it was at the dinner table or a family occasion, there was always a guarantee that the many stories of my grandfather and his father would be told. This book mirrors who my dad is today.

Our grandfather was well respected, which is how we look at our dad. I remember my grandfather vividly, even though I was only seven years old when he passed away. While he faced many challenges, my dad always taught us that we all face tests and trials and must do it with confidence and dedication. My three older sisters and I spent much quality time with our grandfather; my dad is a carbon copy of him in all the best ways.

Jamil

As the only boy in the family, I agree with my sisters that this is a special book because it presents all sides of the stories we have heard our whole lives. We get to see the side of two different generations. I was told that I was only seven months old when I met my grandfather and barely two years old when he passed away. I had never met my grandmother, but having these stories written down is so important to me.

My dad told me about my grandfather's adventures, the type of man he was, how tough he was, and what he experienced in life. My mother told me I am very much like my grandfather because I can be stubborn and hard-headed. My mother agrees that it is "my way or the highway," and often says, "You are just like your grandfather."

Grandfather and Father, circa 1950 (Their first picture taken together)

1

A Paper-Folded Passport
1900-1924

Writing our family history has allowed me to share the background and stories of my grandfather, Ali, and father, Saleh, from Palestine. Their incredible life experiences have played a significant role in shaping who we are today. My inspiration for writing this book comes from reflecting on our family's historical journey. I hope that sharing these stories will provide a better understanding of our ancestors and offer insight into our family's resilience, struggles for survival, and efforts to thrive while preserving our family legacy.

Before we dive into their adventures, let me give you a little background of my childhood in northern Virginia, and then later, beginning to hear the stories my father told about his childhood and my grandfather's adventures when we lived in Rocky Mount, North Carolina. It will help you appreciate how far our family has come.

We lived only a block away from a city park in our neighborhood, where I spent most of my time playing "little league" sports, including baseball, football, and basketball.

It was a great place to grow up, a safe neighborhood where the lights stayed on at night in the city park, which allowed us to be out until 11 p.m. most evenings during the summer months.

Taking the bus to school on the other side of town every morning forced us all to get up early. I went to my first school until sixth grade before transferring to middle school. Public schools throughout North Carolina began busing students in order to desegregate fully.

In 1971, the U.S. Supreme Court ruled in favor of busing as a way to end racial segregation, because African American children were still attending segregated schools. By the 1971–1972 school year, North Carolina had finally satisfactorily met the Supreme Court's Brown decision requirements.

My father, Saleh, owned a small restaurant and bar in the downtown area of Rocky Mount, next to the train station, where many people would stop after work for dinner or a drink. We would go there early on Sunday mornings to help my dad do a weekly deep cleaning of the restaurant. Periodically, we would visit him during business hours, but it was a bar, so we didn't visit that often—it was no place for children. It was called City Lunch, and he did quite well, as he was so close to the train station.

At ten years old, I remember my father telling stories about our family background at social gatherings. One Sunday, when we were home, I was curious about his struggles growing up, so I asked him to tell me about them. I soon realized there was so much to learn that I wished I had recorded them all so I could remember them.

It was a day I will never forget: My dad shared stories about how my grandfather, Ali, was raised. He came across an ID, a paper-folded passport with Grandfather's picture, which stated that he was born in 1900 in Al-Mazara a-Sharqiyah, a small village twenty-five miles northeast of Jerusalem. The village name means *the eastern farm*, and it was only six square miles.

As a side note, *The Paris Times* wrote a story about the village of Al-Mazara a-Sharqiyah when they toured it and labeled it the "Paris of the West Bank" because of all the new construction and growth.

The village is also distinguished by the orchards of olive trees, almond trees, dates, grapes, and lemons, fed by the water flowing from the Wadi Dayqah dam and natural resources. The Ottoman Empire ruled the area until WWI, and its altitude (three thousand feet above sea level) made the lights of Jericho, near the Dead Sea, visible. Jericho is topographically the lowest city on earth (one thousand three hundred feet *below* sea level).

When my great-grandfather decided to remarry, he went to a neighboring village to find his new bride, something considered out of the ordinary at the time. In the late 1800s, it was highly unusual to marry someone outside your own village.

You could say that it was love at first sight, but before a man married a young lady, twenty of the most prominent men in the village had to approve, and a man had to ask the father for his daughter's hand in marriage. Still, most married among their own village, as they were very close-knit tribes.

Around the time my grandfather, Ali, was born, the village's population was 801, with about two hundred homes, buildings, or rooms made of stone and adobe or mud. They weren't mud homes, but they took the dirt, full of minerals, and mixed it with water to create these homes.

If you were to visit the area today, you would still see those homes, some of which have been there for over 150 years. Granted, there are no hurricanes in Palestine, but they do have some intense weather, including hard rainstorms—and snow.

My grandfather had no education. There was no school for him to attend or time for homeschooling. His parents—my great-grandparents—weren't educated either; their only history was what they knew: the Ottomans occupied them, then the British.

My grandfather grew up working in the orchards, wheat fields, and vineyards. Though the vines produced grapes for eating, the leaves were also cooked, stuffed with rice and meat, and eaten. In those days, if they were lucky to have rice, the leaves were cooked in tomato sauce.

Growing up very poor, my grandfather had four siblings, and a half-brother named Muhamad, who was from his father's previous marriage and was ten years older. After his mother passed away, my great-grandfather, also named Saleh, remarried a few years later, and that is when my grandfather was born.

My great-grandfather's name was also Saleh, and he was the oldest son of the new wife. Three more brothers and a sister were born after him.

In 1919, before he turned eighteen, another brother, Isaac, left home to fight in WWI. The family believed he ended up in Italy with the British Forces or Turks, because the Ottomans were in charge, but he never returned. With all the war turmoil in Europe, it was not possible to keep track of missing soldiers, so no one ever knew what happened to him. He had been recruited to fight, and knew it was his only way of getting to live in a different part of the world. At home, there was nothing to do but farm the land, and he was tired of living under the occupation and doing the same thing daily.

Another brother, Omar, fell ill as a teenager and passed away sometime between 1915 and 1917. There was no medicine or doctors to help him back then, and when he got sick, he was bedridden. No one knew what was wrong with him, as it could have been anything.

His sister, Najeeba, never married or had children, and died in the 1930s at a young age, ten years after my father was born. His half-uncle never married either, so my grandfather had four brothers, but three never had children, so the family name did not continue. My grandfather only had my father, and my father's uncle, Domi, had three boys and two girls. That was the extent of the Amra clan.

It was a difficult life for my grandfather growing up in turmoil, losing two of his brothers at an early age, and not much of a future to look forward to or think about. Every day was about surviving and living in a one-room stone dwelling without electricity or running water. His entire life revolved around working the land to grow food.

No doubt, there was bartering between neighbors, but they also had to deal with the government of Ottoman rulers, who would come around and estimate the value of their harvest for the year to determine how much tax they owed. Looking at the size of their property, they would estimate how much was produced and thus gauge what was owed.

Every day, they would get up and work the land, barter among each other, and sell off some of their harvest. Occasionally, they would have eggs from the chickens, and cheese or milk from the goats; they did their best.

My great-uncle, Domi, who raised my father, lived to be 105 years old on a diet of olive oil, figs, and almonds—all organic—along with the natural foods they grew themselves. Back then, chickens weighed about three pounds, not like the mammoth-sized birds you see today in your local grocery store.

They had no medicines or doctors and relied on the food they grew to survive and keep them well. I watched my great-uncle when my great-aunt would make him a breakfast of three eggs cooked in olive oil and served with handmade pita bread, made from the wheat they grew. He fascinated me the few times I visited him in Palestine, and the fact that he had raised my father amazed me even more.

Without any education, living a life of turmoil in an occupied territory was a daily struggle, but that is what made my grandfather who he was. When my father, Saleh, was born, my great-grandfather had already passed away, but my dad has vivid memories of his grandmother, the one who came from a different village.

The British occupation of Palestine was different than the Turkish Ottoman occupation, as the British were mostly blonde and blue-eyed, something the Palestinians were not used to seeing. My grandfather had to find a way to a better life.

My father, Saleh, was born in July 1923, not long after he married my grandmother, Fathia, which means "pure silver." My grandfather, Ali, left home when my father was one year old. He decided to go to South America, where many Middle Easterners traveled to find prosperity and a better way of life for themselves and their families. He knew he would be around familiar customs and traditions. The plan was to go for a couple of years, make money, and then return home. Well, plans change.

2

The Journey Continues
1922-1936

At the ripe old age of ten, I remember so clearly my father sharing the story of his father, my grandfather, at a family function. That was when I learned that my grandfather, Ali, married my grandmother, Fathia, in 1922 in Palestine.

At that time, the English and the French occupied the region, and it was clear that WWI had significantly impacted the economy of Palestine and the entire Middle East. The war disrupted trade and transportation routes, created food shortages, and led to economic decline. Drought, famine, and warfare displaced millions of people, creating the migration and settlement patterns still evident today.

Even though my grandparents were lucky to have chickens for eggs and a goat for milk, they were still repressed, leading my grandfather to pursue a visa to South America. It is remarkable to consider that, for more than its first hundred years, that part of the world had not a single law governing immigration. No federal agency dealing with immigration existed. No visa was required—indeed, the very concept of a visa was unknown. Going to work in South America was as easy as buying a ticket and boarding a ship.

It is possible that my grandfather desired to come to the United States of America. By that time, laws known as the "consular control system" of immigration were established, which divided responsibility for immigration between the State Department and the Immigration and Naturalization Service. It mandated that no person should be allowed to enter the United States without a valid immigration visa issued by an American consular officer abroad.

Consular officers were authorized to issue visas to eligible applicants, but the number of visas that could be issued by each consulate annually was limited, and no more than ten percent of the quota could be given out in any one month. Thus, for the first time, people could not board a ship bound for the U.S. without possessing a valid visa, and therefore, the only option was to go to South America.

Another option would have been to go to Spain, which would have been much easier, because getting documentation was not as complicated. Still, my grandfather got a visitor's visa to go to Venezuela, of which he knew nothing about except that it was a country in South America, with a culture similar to the middle east.

When I looked for the country on a map, I discovered it is situated on major sea and air routes linking North and South America. However, back then, there were no airplanes; people traveled by ship and stopped at ports along the way.

One central landing spot was Havana, Cuba, before Castro took control. My grandfather was supposed to be in Cuba for two weeks while the ship changed crews and passengers before moving on to Venezuela. Before my grandfather got off the ship, he was warned to be very careful, as there were a lot of gangs and violence in Cuba at the time, and he would be looked upon as an outsider.

He got a job in a café, as a busboy, and was allowed to sleep on the ship, but no food or resources were provided, so he had to find a way to survive.

To protect himself, he purchased a small .25 caliber pistol on the black market, which he carried in his pocket. After all, he was a Palestinian in 1924, in an entirely different world, and he had no idea what to expect. There were no informational resources, and he knew nothing about Cuba.

It took thirty days to get to Cuba as a first stop, and while at sea, he built some relationships with others from Palestine.

He was awed because of all the new construction in Cuba that seemed to have a life of its own and with architecture he had never seen before. The structural design of the tall buildings was unique. He'd had nothing to read or look at, no magazines or anything, so he had no idea what the rest of the world looked like. To him, Havana was a happening city with all sorts of activity and movement, with automobiles driving people around. It was crazy to see and very exciting to explore.

After only a week of working, he got into a fight with a co-worker who'd attacked him with a machete. In one full swing, the guy caught the end of my grandfather's thumb and sliced it off. In an effort to defend himself, he pulled out his pistol, shot the guy, and the man went down. Not knowing if the man was dead or what to do, he told some of the people he knew from the ship. When they heard what had happened, they said, "You better run."

The only place he could think of to go was one of the cargo ships docked at the same port as his ship. Unbeknownst to him, the ship was scheduled to leave for New York City the following day. Realizing he had no choice but to blend in, he pretended to be one of the crew, but he had no idea that the distance from Cuba to New York is 1,326 miles, and the voyage would take nine days. He certainly couldn't ask anyone's advice, fearing they would question him and discover what had happened.

When the ship arrived in New York, it wasn't long before the authorities realized he was not on the manifest and asked, "Who are you?"

When they found out he should not have been on the ship, they contacted the Cuban authorities and soon discovered that he was wanted in Cuba for carrying a firearm and shooting a man. They imprisoned him on the cargo ship until they got back to Cuba.

The good news is that the man he shot did not die, but my grandfather still had to stand trial and ended up serving ten months in a Cuban jail because he proved he had acted in self-defense. His proof? Part of his thumb was missing.

By this time, he had been gone from home for quite some time, and his family had no idea where he was. Living conditions in a Cuban prison were horrible, a throwback to the dungeons of centuries ago. The humid cells were filthy and mildewed, with sewage leaks and faulty plumbing. The prison yard was just as bleak and dirty as the cells, and the inmates got no more than an hour of outdoor exercise daily, if they were lucky.

When he finally got out of jail, the authorities said he could not stay in Cuba because he had committed a crime, but he had no desire to stay in Cuba anyway. His original visa was for Caracas, Venezuela, and that's where he wanted to go. So they put him on a ship headed to Caracas, where he knew many Middle Easterners worked and resided.

Sleeping on the ship was quite an adventure and took some getting used to. Each person was assigned a hammock that hung from the ceiling below the deck. It took some skill to climb into that moving hammock each night, but at least he felt safe once he settled in.

However, when the ocean got rough, and the waves grew impossibly high, getting a good night's sleep was impossible. One time, a wave hit the ship, and they were all knocked out of their hammocks. He remembered spending the rest of the night holding onto the one pole going up the middle of the ship near his hammock, praying for the sea to calm.

Grateful to finally arrive in Venezuela safe and sound, he stepped onto land with nothing but the shirt on his back. He learned from other Middle Easterners that there were plentiful agricultural jobs in the area, and, fortunately, a farmer offered him a job as a farmhand. He allowed him to live in the stables, sleep in the hay, and fed him three square meals a day. Mind you, he still had no communication with anyone back home and did not send any money. One year turned into three, four, and five years, but living on the farm allowed him to save what little money he was paid.

My grandfather lived on that farm for ten years. Early on, he met a young lady who lived on the same farm with her family. Her name was Louisa, and he couldn't help but notice her beauty. The minute he saw her, he was intrigued, but also conscious of the fact that he was married and had left behind a wife and child. He never thought he would be there for as long as he was. However, she was very attractive and respectful.

Louisa was picking vegetables from the garden when he first saw her, and when their eyes met, it was an instant attraction. It was the beginning of true love for both of them. Every day, he made a point of looking for her and soon discovered she was a farmhand like him and lived with her family on the farm.

His attraction was a force stronger than the ocean waves, and he didn't mean for their love affair to happen, especially since he had a wife and son back home, but he'd had no communication with them since he had left.

Romance aside, every farmhand had chores to do: milking the cows, gathering eggs, planting seeds, washing clothes, cleaning the outhouse, making soap and candles, and cooking. The different seasons brought their own unique set of chores, activities, and challenges. It wasn't until the automobile came along that their way of life changed, making plowing and other farm chores simpler and more manageable.

However, the farm my grandfather worked on still used the old methods handed down for generations, which meant that, in Venezuela in the 1920s and '30s, modern conveniences were still a long way off. There was no indoor plumbing or electricity, the men delivered ice for the ice boxes, and the livestock and gardens were the primary source of food.

Their story reminds me of the ending scene from the movie *Shawshank Redemption*, when the lead actor says, "Get busy living or get busy dying."

Since they all were farmhands, it was a family-type atmosphere, where most lived in the stables and others stayed in living quarters on the property. It was a farm community of about twenty-five people, and everyone knew everyone else.

My grandfather was a young man of twenty-five, and Louisa was in her early twenties. He never paid attention to any other females on the farm, as she mesmerized him. As their relationship developed and was accepted by everyone, they married around 1935 before leaving the farm together to get a place of their own.

My grandfather tried being a door-to-door salesman. With a suitcase in hand, he went to some Middle Eastern merchants and purchased some inventory to sell, and they also gave him some items on a credit basis.

Back in those days, everyone in the community helped one another, and when he sold what he had, he would go back and pay them and get more merchandise. He worked like this from 1935 to 1941, and did well enough to save even more money and build a nest egg. In 1936, they had a daughter, the first of six children.

In 1941, with an entrepreneurial spirit, he opened his own business, a small shop that sold all sorts of merchandise, from socks to knives to home goods, such as coffee cups, and whatever else anyone needed for the home. It was a small space, but his business took off, and he worked hard with Louisa by his side.

Louisa circa 1949

Ali's business kept growing, so they moved to a bigger space, and by 1945, he was considered a wealthy man. It was then that he built up enough courage to reach out to his loved ones in Palestine. He contacted the Census Bureau in Jerusalem and asked for assistance in locating the family he had left behind in 1924. Though it took courage, he was still a little fearful because he was now married again with six children.

He was forty-five years old and had been away for twenty-one years. He naturally wondered if the wife, son, and siblings he'd left behind were still there. It ate at him emotionally and psychologically, but he was afraid to mention anything about his new family.

Back then, it was common for men to leave their

families, but they often would not make any money or fail at their ventures. Many men would go to Spain and South America and would never be heard from again. The people left behind figured their men did not survive the trip or didn't have enough money to return home. Some men adopted an entirely new lifestyle and had no desire to go back home.

As you can imagine, it was quite a shock that he would want to communicate with the family he'd abandoned after twenty-one years, but he was an honorable man and wanted a relationship with his son. Besides, he had a natural curiosity about the other members of his family.

3

Way of Life
1923-1948

Meanwhile, my father, Saleh, was still a young boy living in Palestine with the head of the family, his father's brother, Uncle Domi. Domi was quite hard on him as he was growing up, and his mother, Fathia, had to obey his uncle's harsh commands. Mentally and emotionally abusive, he made my father quit school in the third grade because, in his mind, my father was old enough to work.

As a young boy, my father had to work the fields and care for the livestock daily. That was his life—they had no money to send him to school or to buy school supplies.

"All that costs money," his uncle said.

Part of my great-uncle's reasoning was that if his own children could not go to school, why should his nephew be allowed to attend school? It turns out he had feelings of animosity toward my father because he'd had to take care of him since my grandfather had shirked his duty.

Those negative feelings prevented my father from having a relationship with his uncle, and the way he treated

Fathia like a second-class citizen only added to his agony and resentment. It was almost too much for him to bear. However, his mother did not want to leave his uncle's house and disrupt her son's life.

Back then, if a woman left her family, she could not take her son with her, and Fathia couldn't endure the thought of leaving my father behind. She felt terrible that her son had to wear shoes made from tire treads with ties that wrapped around his ankle, but she put up with Uncle Domi's abuse to stay by her son.

In 1936, Domi went to Spain for six months, and when he returned, Fathia was surprised to see that he had bought my father his first pair of shoes. My father was surprised, too, but he would take anything he could get out of his uncle.

Grandmother Fathia

Everything about my father's childhood seemed normal, as that was all he knew. For instance, leaving the village and going on a trip to Jerusalem for a visit was something he would have enjoyed doing, but that was out of the question. It would have been hard to make that trip without the resources.

All he knew was that he was an only child, and his father was gone. All he had for male role models were his uncle Domi and an older uncle, Mohammed, who wasn't around much either. He was very respectful of his mother, and though his cousins were a tad younger than him, they were like siblings to him.

My grandmother, Fathia, was from the Shatara family, and she had one brother, my father's uncle, who was considered the patriarch of the Shatara family. My father didn't have much of a relationship with this uncle either, since he was busy with a large family of his own. He wished he could have known his uncle better, but the opportunity never materialized.

The one uncle, Domi, was all my father knew while growing up. He didn't have anyone to nurture, guide, or teach him how to be a man. His uncle was only concerned with him when it was time to work the land, and he often felt intimidated by his uncle because of the way he was treated. Imagine living in a one-room home with no indoor plumbing or electricity, and the only heat or light comes from kerosene lamps. It would get cold in the wintertime in Palestine, and though they had a well for water, bathing was not a routine occurrence for my father as a kid.

As my father grew older, he had two relatives he ran around with, Thaher and Azziz. They were from the same tribe and were considered distant cousins, but they became his running buddies—if he raised any Cain, he raised it with them.

There were no books to read, and, of course, no school. It wasn't a requirement for kids to go to school; it was more valuable for them to work the land with their family. Because it was a small village, there were few children, and everyone was more focused on survival, rather than education.

When children did attend school, no matter what age, they all gathered in one room. It was like in the Laura Ingalls Wilder era, where reading, writing, and arithmetic were taught in one little schoolhouse. The only books involved in his education were what the teacher had on hand, such as a history or math book. The teacher would lecture, and, with pencil and paper, they would write down their lessons, and this is how they learned to read, write, and do arithmetic.

For fun, they played soccer whenever they could. They formed athletic teams that provided a social, national, and institutional base for Palestine's political organization in the first half of the twentieth century. In the 1930s, some men who had made it out of the village played soccer for the Palestine Football Federation, and they would come back with stories. That is how the kids in the village learned what soccer was all about, and it gave them something to dream about, people to admire, and allowed them to imagine a way out for themselves.

Outside of school, they had no balls to play with, so they got creative and made balls out of yarn rolled up to the size of a softball. They determined who the best hitter was by how far they could hit the yarn ball. That was their life: working the fields, learning about soccer, and playing baseball with a yarn ball.

From the 1920s through the late 1940s, Palestine was occupied, and there was always a British military presence. Occupation was a way of life, and they knew nothing else. My father never told me about any children in the village being abused by the military, but they all knew there had to be something better.

My father and grandmother lived in a single 10 by 12 room in his uncle's L-shaped complex, which had three rooms total, plus an outhouse. Uncle Domi built another room next to theirs, which he turned into a grocery store with the money he'd earned in Spain. That was the first time my father recognized that there was such a thing as entrepreneurship— in other words, he realized that they could do more than just farm. There was another way to generate a living, and at a young age, he watched that happen.

After a while, the grocery store concept turned into a bakery, and my father watched as a 10 by 8 room morphed into a full-blown business. Although he didn't see eye to eye with his uncle, what he learned from him about business helped shape his career later in life.

Meanwhile...

For years, his mother thought that her husband (my grandfather) would return, but eventually, she gave up hope of that happening. After all, twelve years had passed since he'd left. But her devotion to my father, who was developing into a young man, never wavered.

Grandfather, Ali Amra 1950

Of course, he faced some challenges as a teenager, as he could be quite stubborn, especially as he filled out physically. Then, he was no longer intimidated by his uncle, although he wore a gown known as a *gallabiyah*, instead of a shirt and trousers, and makeshift shoes, and once my father realized that his father was never coming back, he knew he would have to be the man of the family. He believed there was a way to make a better life, and he never lost his confidence or felt sorry for himself. He became self-assured and developed quite a presence when he walked into a room.

On a side note, over the years, people have said, "Your dad was a lot taller than you, wasn't he?" And my response is always the same: "No, he was the same height as me." What people mean is that his *persona* was larger than life. All the trials and tribulations he faced growing up, along with what he experienced as a young man, made him that way.

He was sixteen years old when he noticed a posting at city hall. The police were recruiting officers. He'd never thought about becoming a police officer, but when he saw the posting, it hit him that this could be his way out. This position would allow him to create a future for himself and his mother, no matter the repercussions. That sparked a burning desire inside him, and he decided to pursue it.

He held on to that thought as time passed, but still worked the fields with his uncle. His oldest cousin ran the bakery, and it became commonplace for women to bring their bread dough there to bake it, which saved them the trouble of baking it at home. Women would bring in a big tub of dough, and workers at the bakery would chop it up and make individual pita breads. This is how the bakery thrived and became quite successful.

The Uprising

Then, in 1936, the anti-occupation riots rocked Palestine. The Arab Revolt was instigated by a massive influx of Jewish immigrants, partly due to the rise of Nazism in pre-war Germany. Following increased tensions and a number of violent incidents perpetrated by both Palestinians and Jews, rioting erupted on April 19, 1936, in Jaffa and Tel Aviv, quickly spreading throughout Palestine and resulting in the killing of several Jews and Palestinians. An extensive general strike was declared, and other forms of political protest, such as non-payment of taxes, led by an Arab Higher Committee, were presided over by Jerusalem Mufti Hajj Amin al-Hussein.

In addition to the political protests, both Palestinian- and Jewish-farmed orchards were destroyed, and both

Palestinian and Jewish civilians were murdered. The goals of the revolt were to shift British policy by limiting or ending large-scale Jewish immigration, to ban further land sales to Jews, and to enable Palestinians to establish their own national government.

Britain established the Peel Commission to investigate the rebellion, which recommended the partition of Palestine into two states (one Arab and one Jewish), with a retained British mandate in Bethlehem, Nazareth, and Jerusalem, and a corridor from Jerusalem to the sea. The Commission's recommendation of partition (though not the boundaries proposed) was accepted at the 20th Zionist Congress (in part because it called for the transfer of Palestinians from the designated Jewish state to the designated Arab state, which many leading Zionists advocated), but the Arab Higher Committee rejected it, leading to a resumption of the revolt, which then targeted British forces militarily. Harsh British measures, including exiling many Palestinian leaders, disbanding the Arab Higher Committee, and establishing military courts, ultimately suppressed the riots.

After that, life was different in more ways than one. No citizen was allowed to own a firearm, but many men kept rifles hidden in their homes, just in case. However, those rifles were no match for the weaponry of the British military. One day, a group of about thirteen men were caught, surrendered, and lined up to be killed. My father was only thirteen years old at the time and was forced to watch these men, whom he knew well, be executed. The British Forces spared my father's life because he was a young boy, and so he was able to walk away, but it certainly left him in shock.

As the British forces walked off, one man, who was still barely alive, tapped my father on the leg, motioning him to bend down so he could tell him something. Barely able to speak, he said he knew the British would be patrolling the entire village to see if anyone had more weapons. If they went to his home, they might discover the rifles he had hidden and kill his whole family. "My rifles are hidden in the hay behind the house. Please run and tell my wife where they are, so she can get rid of them," the man said, barely able to get the words out.

Nodding, my father said to him, "I will; don't worry," as the man died before his very eyes. My father ran off to locate the man's wife, so he could share what had happened and warn her. The British were in the process of searching everyone's homes, and he knew it would be certain death for her and anyone in the home if they discovered those hidden rifles.

Following the April rioting in June 1936, which resulted in the killing of sixteen Jews and five Palestinians, the British, in an attempt to pacify the Palestinian Arabs, collaborated with Transjordan, Iraq, Saudi Arabia, and Egypt. However, by the end of September 1936, 20,000 British troops in Palestine had been deployed to "round up Arab bands," and on October 9, the rulers ordered the strike to end.

My father told me that, during this time, he barely had anything to eat on a daily basis and was always hungry. In fact, even to have an egg was a big deal. Since he was so hungry all the time, he would sneak into the bakery in the middle of the night and eat whatever he could get his hands on, opening up cans of sardines or boxes of candy or whatever he could find. Keeping himself hidden, he had to make sure not to leave a trace that he had been in the bakery. There was a deep shelf above one of the walls, and he would throw the wrappers and empty cans up there, knowing there would be hell to pay if he got caught. Years later, when they were tearing down that building, all those empty cans and wrappers came tumbling down.

Father, circa 1941

In 1941, when my father turned eighteen, he heard the British were finally recruiting for the Palestinian police force. They were riding through the villages, announcing they would be back to recruit potential candidates. The requirements were that men had to be 172 centimeters (at least 5 feet 8) and be able to read and write a little bit.

Though my father only had a third-grade education, he was the right height, so he applied. He thought it would be a miracle if he got picked, so he left and returned to working the fields, plowing the ground behind two mules. When he told others he had applied to be a police officer, they looked down on him, as if he would be working for the enemy. But he thought it would be a way to protect his family, as well as other Palestinians, and a way to provide a better life for him and his mother. Besides, he never thought he would get accepted.

Months went by, and one day, while he was working in a wheat field in a valley, he heard someone yelling his name. "Saleh—the British Police are looking for you."

My father had given up being accepted into the British Police, even though he had applied, but immediately, he dropped his plow and ran off, jumping and screaming for joy, realizing he had been recruited. His uncle called him crazy as he was running off. Despite his limited education, he was absolutely thrilled to be called for service in the British Police Force. For him, it was like winning the lottery.

His mom, Fathia, cried and yelled to him as he ran off, "You are going to go and not come back like your father."

As he passed by them to leave, he was so angry and frustrated at having had to endure life without a father that he said, "Listen, I am going to make a better life for myself and you."

"But will I ever see you again?" she cried.

He said, "I am going to make something of my life. If you think I'm going to work behind a plow for the rest of my life, that is not happening. Besides, under our circumstances, we will never have our own way of life."

She hung her head in sadness and replied, "I know."

He continued and said, "I am going to go make a better life for us."

It didn't matter what his mother said—he was done. He washed up, put on his traditional abaya, and ran to the village where the British were verifying applicants. They told him he had been chosen for the police force and would have to report for basic training the next day at a base an hour away.

He didn't have a car or truck, so he hitched a ride and slept at a bus stop to be on time the next day, when he met with British authorities and was told he would go to the Gaza Strip for basic training. He knew he had to do this. Going through basic training with the grueling physical requirements was no picnic, but he made it through and became a cop on horseback, known as the mounted police.

He was gone from home for about eight months, and no one knew where he was. When he finally had three days off, he returned home, riding into town on his horse in full uniform, holding a rifle. Now considered a hometown hero, everyone came out to welcome him home.

Father, circa 1943

His mother was thrilled to see him and felt so proud. They had not seen each other for months, and it took her a few seconds to realize it was her son in a police uniform. After everyone greeted him with open arms, he went home with his mother to discuss his accomplishments.

When they sat at the table, he looked at her and asked, "How much money did you make from the entire harvest this year?"

"I made eighty denars," she replied.

That would be about $120, a good amount in the early 1940s. He then pulled out a wad of money from his pocket and handed her a total of 400 denars.

Her eyes went wide with shock. "Did you steal this? Who did you rob?" she asked.

Laughing, he said, "No—this is the money I made from my sweat and tears working with the British Police Force."

She was shocked, but at the same time, proud of her son, who had done so well, and she was grateful that he'd come home.

4

Police Force Adventures
1941-1949

Before we get into what happened when he went to see his father in the next chapter, let me share some of the amazing stories he experienced as a police officer working for the British military.

You may recall how my father got recruited into the police force, which meant working for the British military. Initially, his family and friends looked down upon him for taking such a position and working for the occupiers. However, he looked at the situation as a way to protect his family and his village by being a Palestinian under British command. Besides, he no longer wanted to live under his uncle's rule. He wanted to give himself an opportunity for a brighter future. When he joined the police force, he was trained to become a mounted policeman, which was much more prestigious than being a policeman on foot patrol.

That was the beginning of his relationship with horses. He loved them. Even if he watched the Kentucky Derby, it wasn't because he was interested in the race, it was more about seeing the beautiful horses. When the opportunity arose, he was always up for a horseback ride. Even if we weren't with him, he would take time to ride a horse any chance he could.

In his eyes, working for the British military as a Palestinian would help protect his family, so he rode those coattails for the duration of his time in the police force. During his service as a mounted policeman, he did what he could to protect those he knew in any of the villages that they patrolled.

While he was on duty, the British military would go to towns and villages, searching home by home, for weapons. It was illegal to be in possession of a weapon of any kind, and if anyone was found with a weapon, they would be jailed or possibly even executed.

One night, they arrived at a home where a husband, wife, and three small children lived. Most homes had only one or two rooms. The animals would stay in one, and everyone else lived in the other. Usually, there would be a space above those rooms to store food and necessities for everyone, including the animals.

While searching their one little room, he was told by his commanding officer to go up to the second level. Gingerly, he climbed up a ladder and searched with his hands. There was a stack of hay in the middle of the shelf, and when he reached his arm into the middle of that hay, he felt what could only be a rifle.

Keeping his cool, he looked down to see if anyone was watching, and all he could see was the husband and wife looking at him with fear in their eyes as they turned pale as ghosts. He slowly held his finger to his lips for them to be quiet, then slowly descended the ladder. He reported that all was clear, and he could see the couple breathe a sigh of relief. They knew that he had saved the husband from being taken away or both of them being executed.

After a few weeks, a package from those villagers arrived at his station house. It contained fresh homemade goat cheese, and a small metal can of homemade olive oil. Since the package had no sender's name, he thought back to that couple and was sure that this was a token of their appreciation.

Another time, he was in his home village and was called to go to the house of someone who had heard gunshots. It turned out that the person was his close relative, who was in a dispute with his brother-in-law over some land. Sure enough, the brother-in-law had gone to his relative's house to kill him. When my father rode up to the house on his horse, he dismounted and pulled his rifle from his saddle. Through the front window, he could see a man aiming a rifle at someone he couldn't see. He didn't want to kill the man, so he aimed his rifle toward the house, close to the front window, and fired a warning shot. It was enough to let them know he was there, and immediately, the man dropped his rifle and jumped out a back window. My father knew who the man was and could have gone after him, but that would have been a disaster for that entire family, if he caught and arrested him.

Fortunately, he was alone and on leave at that time, but he found the guy the next day and said to him, "You are going to resolve this situation peacefully, or I will go to the British authorities, and at the very least, they will arrest you. Either way, you won't see your family ever again."

The man agreed to resolve the issue peacefully. My father earned a lot of credibility with the people of his village because he took that approach in many situations that he was confronted with.

To the British, the most-wanted guy in all of Palestine was a man called Fareed Shalaby, known by even the highest military commander in Palestine; that is how badly they wanted this guy. As far as they were concerned, he was a terrorist, and they wanted him out of the territory.

A rebel in every sense of the word, Fareed was always up to something and did all sorts of things to disrupt what the British were doing. Fareed was related to my father and was from his village, so the head of the British military in the region, Commander Ford, requested that my father meet with him. Obviously, my father was shocked, but he had no choice. He sat down with Commander Ford, who immediately asked him, "What is your relationship with Fareed?"

"Well, he is from my hometown and a distant relative, but I am not close to him at all," my father replied. "I haven't seen him since I have been on the police force."

"He is the most-wanted man in the area, and I require you to apprehend him, if the opportunity presents itself," Ford said sternly.

"Yes, sir. I understand," my father replied.

Having made his intentions clear, Ford said, "I want you to go back to your village and find a way to meet with Fareed peacefully. Make sure he understands that there is no chance of him being ambushed or apprehended by British authorities, if he accepts your invitation to meet with him."

My father sat there looking a bit confused when the commander pulled a bag out of the cabinet with a wrapped box of some sort inside. He had no idea what was in the box, but Ford instructed him to give it to Fareed as a gift. My father was given a three-day leave in order to find and arrange a meeting with Fareed.

The commander said, "Let him know he cannot continue doing what he is doing. If he gives himself up now, we will be much more lenient, but if we catch him, he will be executed. If he surrenders, we will not kill him. Either he can leave the territory completely or give himself up."

My father returned to his hometown and sent word throughout the village that he wanted to meet with Fareed, with full assurance that no harm would come to him. He told many village men, "Someone must know where he is, and I need to meet with him, no strings attached. He doesn't have to worry about being ambushed. I have a message for him from Commander Ford."

After word got out, Fareed sent a message that he would meet him in the Mukhtar's (head of the village) office in the village. It had to be in the middle of town where there were people around, not a private place. They set a time to meet at the Mukhtar's office, where they sat down over tea.

My father had the bag with the wrapped box inside and said, "The commander told me to speak with you to plead with you to turn yourself in. If you don't, they will find you and execute you. In fact, he gave me this to give you as a gift."

Fareed looked at the bag and couldn't imagine what was inside. A little bit hesitant, he took the package out of the bag, opened it up. Inside the box was a brand-new pair of boots and a letter that read:

Fareed—

We know that all your running around has worn out your boots. Here is a new pair for you. If you continue to run, know that you will meet your final fate if you choose this route.

Commander Ford

Fareed was excited about his brand-new boots, which were similar to the boots the British military wore; sure enough, his old boots were worn out.

Immediately, he took his old boots off, put them in the box, and said to my father, "Give the box back to the commander, but I will never give up and never stop doing what I am doing."

My father took the package and returned to his post to meet with Commander Ford.

When he saw him with the package in his hand, Ford asked, "Did you meet with him?"

"Oh yes, I did," he replied. "He asked me to return this package to you."

The commander opened the box, giggled when he saw Fareed's old pair of boots inside, and said, "Okay—you did your job, and now we know what we have to do."

In order to pursue Fareed, they searched out who they could bribe in the village, someone close to Fareed, to give them specific information that would help capture him. Persistent in their quest to find that person, they recruited and convinced Fareed's sister's husband.

Fareed's sister was just as rebellious about the occupation as Fareed was, but the British found a way to get to her husband. In fact, the only people Fareed trusted were his sister and his brother-in-law. As soon as the opportunity presented itself, they bribed the husband to find and kill Fareed.

When Fareed came to town, he always slept under trees in the pastures in hidden areas and would send for his brother-in-law. At this particular time, when they were united, Fareed said, "I am tired of being on the run, but I have to get some rest. Can you watch over things while I sleep? Here is my gun."

The brother-in-law waited until Fareed was sound asleep, pulled the gun out of his pocket, and shot him in the head, then immediately took off. As he ran back to the village, he thought of what he was going to say to everyone about what had happened, and decided to say that the British had ambushed them and that they had shot Fareed.

For a while, everyone believed that story. However, Fareed's sister became increasingly suspicious of his story because now, all of a sudden, her husband had money and their way of life was changing. She wasn't buying it and decided to investigate the surroundings where it happened. Of course, back then, they didn't have forensics to determine what went on, but she was not convinced that the British killed Fareed because they would have made a spectacle of him to the entire village. With time, she put two and two together and soon realized that her husband had killed her brother.

Her husband listened to what she had to say and pleaded with her. "They were going to kill him anyway, and look at all this money we got! We can do all sorts of things that we could never do before with this money."

Originally, she had no idea that the British paid him to kill her brother, but could not bear that her husband had done such a thing. She played along with it for a while, then plotted to shoot and kill her husband to avenge her brother's death.

That ended the Fareed legacy. The British accomplished what they wanted, and he was finally out of their hair. Of course, there were others to pursue, but no one like him. He was considered just like one of the FBI's most-wanted men in today's world. When she shot her husband, she went on the run, and the British and the local authorities started looking for her. Eventually, she passed away somewhere in southern Lebanon.

Until my father's inability to speak due to dementia, the one thing he could still remember in great detail were the stories about his police work. Those eight years in the Palestinian Police Force under the British command were the most enjoyable and memorable of his life. I do not doubt that those eight years shaped his view of the world, and it shaped his character and motivation to have a better life. Being a police officer taught him the value of time management, organization, and self-care. In addition, his time in the police force gave him the equivalent of a college education.

Looking back, I can remember my father's ability to speak the sophisticated Arabic language with a unique, complicated dialect led him to become a news broadcaster after he left the police force. However, his career in broadcasting was short-lived because he decided to go to Venezuela to find his father.

To make some extra cash to fund his trip, he bought a little 1949 white pickup truck with the money he had earned while in the police force. Back then, all cars were either white or black. However, since horses were the main form of transportation, my father had never learned to drive a car. So he hired one of the older men in the village who drove the village bus to teach him how to drive.

Then my father realized that the small bus could only hold so many people, so he offered to load people into the bed of his pickup truck, and they paid him for a ride to Ramallah, the administrative capital of Palestine and a flourishing city with a large marketplace. He did that for a living, along with broadcasting, while he earned enough to visit his father.

5

Traveling to Venezuela
1949-1953

An older generation of Israelis and Palestinians, including my father, can still remember British soldiers patrolling the streets of Palestine, Jerusalem, Tel Aviv, and Ramallah during the three decades that Britain controlled the territory. British troops captured Jerusalem from the Ottoman Empire in 1917, and in 1922, the League of Nations awarded Britain an international mandate to manage and control Palestine during the post-war deal-making that resulted in the map of the Middle East being redrawn. Exhausted by WWII and dealing with the strain of keeping Jewish and Arab

My father's passport picture circa 1949

43

forces apart, the British military withdrew in 1948. When the British military pulled out of Palestine, which then became part of Jordan, my father decided to retire from the police force, and thought it was a perfect time to visit his father.

Meanwhile, at this point, no one knew if my grandfather, Ali, was still alive, and Ali wondered if his family still existed in Palestine. He sent his family a letter through the census bureau in Jerusalem. My grandmother told my father that the letter was from his father, my grandfather, but they ignored it. When my grandfather received no response, he asked the census bureau if the letter had been delivered, and they said it had. He decided to write another letter, only this time, he put a check for $500 in the envelope.

My father and grandmother were stunned when that letter arrived with a check for $500, and soon realized it was from my grandfather, who was obviously still alive. This occurred in 1945, meaning twenty-one years had elapsed since Ali had left his wife and son.

The family was shocked when his letter arrived. Back in those days, my grandmother could have chosen to go back to her family when her husband left, but if she had done that, she would have had to give up her son. So she chose to live a single life, raising her son under the authority of an abusive man, even though it was psychologically traumatic for my father.

The whole family thought my father was out of his

mind when he said he wanted to go to Venezuela to see his father, but he was determined. He reached out to his father and said, "I am coming to see you."

"No, you can't come here," his father said. "Take care of your mom, and I will keep sending you money."

Refusing to take no for an answer, he replied, "No, I am coming, whether you help me or not."

My grandfather had not told my father about his new family, so he worried about his son's reaction. My father needed a visa to go to Venezuela, but at that point, my grandfather refused to get one for him. Somehow, my father managed to get a tourist visa to Brazil, and when he arrived there, he sent word to his father that he was in Brazil and that, one way or another, he would ultimately get to Venezuela on his own, if he did not help him.

Finally, my grandfather gave in and said, "Let me work on a visa for you to get here."

While my father was waiting for the documents to be completed, he lived in a hotel for ninety days. His daily schedule consisted of getting up every morning, eating breakfast, then walking to the local movie theater and watching movies all day until it was time to return to the hotel, eat dinner, and go to bed. You might be wondering why he was doing this, and when asked, he said, "I didn't know anyone there and was all alone—what better way to use the time to learn a different language than to watch movies?" It gave him a sense of knowing more about the culture.

Meanwhile, my grandfather was working on getting the documents for my father to get a visa, and, sure enough, after ninety days, it was complete and my father was prepared to travel from Brazil to Caracas, Venezuela. My father was supposed to arrive on a certain day but arrived two days early. Since he had my grandfather's business address, he turned up at the front entrance to his business and left his bags outside. When he walked into my grandfather's clothing store, he saw all sorts of apparel and fabrics, and several employees walking around helping customers. He saw a gentleman standing behind the counter dressed in a neatly pressed white suit, and immediately knew it was his dad. Even though they didn't have any pictures of each other, he had a general idea of what his father would look like.

When he saw my father, my grandfather spoke to him in Spanish and, not knowing who he was, treated him like a customer, asking, "How can I help you today?"

My father spoke to him in Arabic and said, "I am here to see a friend—Saleh."

He smiled and said, "That is my son. He will be here in a couple of days. Come sit over here and let me get you a cup of coffee."

Sitting down at a table in the corner of the store, they chatted about things in general, and then my grandfather proceeded to share how much he was looking forward to seeing his son. He went into great detail about how he had left him when he was only a year old, and told him the whole story, where he had gone, and the adventures he had been through.

After about forty-five minutes, my father stopped him, looked into my grandfather's eyes, and said, "I am him. I am my father's son."

In total shock, my grandfather started to shake uncontrollably, and then he slowly stood, holding onto the table, and teared up. My father thought he was going to fall over and immediately grabbed him to give him a big hug. The employees were freaking out a bit because they thought something was terribly wrong. In fact, one of the employees called the police for some help.

When my grandfather heard them calling the authorities, he knew he had to gather himself and said, "Tell them—it is okay—tell them this is my son."

The authorities had already been called, and when they showed up, my grandfather had to tell the whole story to them, and then introduced my father, his son, to everyone, saying, "I haven't seen him since he was one year old."

In the district where his store was located were many Middle Easterners who had come from Syria, Lebanon, Egypt, and Jordan to find work. My grandfather went out into the streets and called out to everyone to come and meet his son. Before they knew it, the gathering in the store turned into a big celebration, and they spent the rest of the afternoon enjoying some good food and drink while getting acquainted.

With so many people around, my father had not had a chance to tell my grandfather what his life had been like, and when the afternoon festivities ended, it was time to close up shop and call it a day. Together, they checked on the rest of my grandfather's businesses before getting in the car to drive home.

While driving, my grandfather said, "Listen, my son—I have to tell you why I hesitated for you to come here. To be honest, I was afraid."

"Why were you afraid?" my father asked.

"Because I am married and have six children. You have six siblings—four sisters and two brothers."

At first, my father was a little taken aback when he learned about his new family and took some time to gather his thoughts. After thinking about what my grandfather must have gone through, it made sense that he did what he did, because he had been gone for twenty-six years and worked hard to establish a new life. After much thought, it really was not that surprising that he'd remarried and started a family.

"I understand," my father replied after he gathered himself.

At that point, my grandfather was comfortable going home, and when they arrived at his large home and walked through the front door, my grandfather's wife, Louisa, greeted my father with open arms and welcomed him like a prince. My grandfather had called ahead and told her what had happened, so she had prepared a big feast to make him feel comfortable and part of the family. All his sisters and brothers started coming in, ranging in age from the oldest daughter, Sensione, who was eleven years old, to the youngest, who was four years old. To make him feel even more welcome, Louisa prepared a room for him, and as he settled in, he became part of that family quite easily. Yet, in his mind, he was only there to convince his father to return to the Middle East if, for nothing else, to visit his mother and the remainder of the family.

However, once my father realized the situation and actually saw what his father, my grandfather, had created, living in a beautiful home with a nice car and all the businesses he built, he knew his father had no interest in returning to the Middle East when he was entrenched in such a wonderful lifestyle. A year flew by, and my father realized that my grandfather had become more South American than Palestinian. At this point, my father felt that he needed to convince his father to at least go back for a visit and to see the wife, brothers, and extended family he had left behind.

My father implored him, saying, "You need to go back to your village and your family, even if it is just for a visit."

"No," my grandfather said, adamantly against it. "There is no chance in hell that I could make that trip. I live a modern lifestyle here, and you expect me to return to where they take baths in a barrel?"

Still determined, my father kept chipping away at

him to get him to visit and said, "I understand that you don't want to go back there and live your life; just go and get reacquainted with everyone you left behind. My mother has waited for you since the day you left. Don't you owe her a visit?"

He kept badgering my grandfather, so their discussions would get quite heated. There was a time when my grandfather got so frustrated with my father that he punched him in the nose. One of their close friends happened to be in the store when that happened, and saw my father fall to the ground. The Lebanese friend helped my father get up off the floor, and as he lifted him up, he looked at my father and said, "Don't you dare strike your father back."

"No, of course not," my father replied. "I would not do that."

That incident triggered my grandfather to rethink going back to his village because he so regretted that he had struck his son after all the years of not being there for him. Here, his son had become successful in the police force without any help from him, and they'd had an altercation.

He thought, Maybe I need to make this trip.

The decision wasn't immediate; it still took another year, but that's when he turned the corner and started asking his son more about the village and how his other relatives were doing.

My father told him about one relative, Abu Elouf,

who was a medicine man. Abu was considered a master healer and successfully treated people with natural herbs and tinctures. My grandfather was so intrigued by this story because Abu was a teenager when he'd last seen him.

In later years, Abu Elouf became known as a medical miracle worker who provided quick solutions for problems. In fact, when Jordan's King Hussein developed a rash on his face that no doctor could heal, he sent word to the village people of Al-Mazra'a, where Abu lived, saying that he would like the medicine man to visit him at the palace. The king even sent the Jordanian military police to fetch him. One officer said, "The king kindly requests your presence at the palace."

"He wants me to go to the palace?" Abu Elouf asked.

"Yes, he is asking you to come."

Abu went to see the king, and when he found out what the problem was, he developed an herbal remedy that healed the king's face. The king was so grateful for finding relief from his rash that he agreed to pay him regularly for the rest of his life.

My grandfather was fascinated by this story and many other tales that his son told him about the people in his village, and he finally, after three years, said to his son, "I will go back."

But my grandfather said, "There is one other major issue."

"What is that?" my father asked.

"How am I going to go? I have no identification or

official Palestinian documentation," he said.

Back then, in Venezuela, there was no permanent residency identification needed, as long as you didn't do anything illegal or anti-government. My grandfather had built a life and existed this whole time without any Venezuelan permanent residency status.

"I have no way to travel," he said.

My father gave that some thought and remembered that one of their friends was a Syrian gentleman who worked at the Syrian Embassy. My father said, "Let's go and ask our friend if he can help us."

When they located this gentleman at his office, my father gestured to my grandfather and said to the man, "This man left Palestine in 1924 and would like to go back for a visit."

After learning more about the situation and taking his picture, the Embassy man said, "Give me a few days."

My father and grandfather left and returned home. A few days later, the Syrian man sent word for them to come to his office. When they got there, the Syrian gentleman opened his desk drawer and gave my grandfather a Syrian passport and visa. He said, "Here you go. You are officially a Syrian citizen and can fly into Damascus. Your family can meet you at the airport in Syria, and when you are ready to leave, make sure you leave from Syria because you are considered a Syrian resident with this passport."

My father and grandfather thanked him profusely and left in disbelief. As they walked out of the Embassy, my grandfather said, "Well, that solved that problem."

"You're right. Now, it is time to figure out how we are to go on this trip," my father said.

They discovered my grandfather could fly, though he would have to make several stops along the way. My grandfather had to prepare himself, as this would be his first time on a plane and first trip back to the Middle East. Talk about a new adventure!

So they packed their suitcases, and together, they flew into Damascus after sending word by telegram to my grandfather's brother, Domi, and my grandmother, saying they were coming.

My grandmother, an incredible woman, had the wherewithal to realize that my grandfather would get off the plane dressed like an American, in a suit and tie. He should be wearing a traditional Palestinian abaya, a cloak made from fine, high-quality fabric, over his shirt and pants, along with a headdress.

My grandmother took the abaya and headdress with her to meet him at the airport, and as soon as he got off the plane, she walked right up to him without even saying hello and demanded, "Take off your jacket and hat."

She flung the hat, a fedora, in the air as if it were a frisbee, and as soon as he removed his jacket, she did the same with it.

"Now, take off that tie," she commanded, flinging that in the air, too. She opened the bag she had brought with her and said, "Put this on," handing him the headdress and the abaya. "This is how you will arrive to see your people in the village for the first time," she said.

It had been twenty-eight years since my grandfather had left his village, and he was shocked to see the busloads of townspeople who had come to meet him at the airport in Damascus to welcome him home. They all got on the buses and drove back to Al-Mazra'a. When they arrived, it was an all-out party, a celebration, like the 4th of July. People had to wrap their minds around the fact that my grandfather had been gone since 1924—and it was now 1952. They looked at him like a hero because he returned after being gone so long. If it weren't for my father, who insisted that he go back for a visit, my grandfather would never have known how thrilled the people of his village were to see him, and the fact that they had not forgotten him. My grandfather felt so honored by their warmth and hospitality.

The people of his village lived a simple life, and my grandfather noticed that nothing much had changed since he had been gone. People still lived off the land, and there was no economy to speak of, but it was a very calm and peaceful way of living. At that point, they needed to celebrate an event like my grandfather coming back to help them forget how much they'd lost during the British occupation.

The fact is, in 1948, over 500 Palestinian villages were destroyed and more than three-quarters of historic Palestine was occupied. This is known as the Nakba, which means catastrophe in Arabic, and refers to the mass displacement and dispossession of Palestinians during the Arab Israeli war of 1948. Before the Nakba, Palestine was a multi-ethnic and multi-cultural society. After it, the majority of the Palestinian population was banished and displaced.

This is significant because Palestine is considered the Holy Land for Christians, the birthplace of Jesus of Nazareth, and the site of his ministry. For Muslims, Jerusalem's Dome of the Rock marks the spot from which the Prophet Mohammed is said to have ascended to heaven. It is also known as the birthplace of Judaism.

Three of the world's major religions—the monotheist traditions of Judaism, Christianity, and Islam—were all born in the Middle East and are all inextricably linked to one another. Christianity was born from within the Jewish tradition, and Islam developed from Christianity and Judaism.

So, how long did my grandfather stay?

6

Grandfather's Stay
1952-1958

The intention was that my grandfather, Ali, would visit his village and family for three months, while my father, Saleh, who was more than willing, would go back and take care of the family and all the businesses since no one else could do that. After all, Louisa was busy caring for six children and meeting their daily demands. My father was happy to do it, since he had been the one to badger my grandfather into making the trip.

That journey began with my grandfather getting reacclimated and reacquainted with everyone he had left behind and had

Grandparents with brother Jad / first picture taken together after my grandfather's return in 1952

not seen for twenty-eight years. My grandmother had waited all those years, not expecting to see him again, although she was fully committed to raising her son, even if it meant doing it on her own. Of course, they needed time to get to know each other again. Plus, he had to get reacquainted with the relatively primitive way of life, which, at the time, made him miss his luxury lifestyle back in Venezuela.

Grandfather Ali spent the first thirty days getting reacquainted with his brother and other relatives, who showed him the land they had cultivated and what they had been doing with their lives to survive and raise their families under strenuous conditions. They hoped my grandfather could use his money to expand the properties they owned, thinking he would be able to visit periodically. My grandfather started thinking about his future and what he could accomplish in his homeland. Though he had planned to stay for only ninety days, he adapted to his old lifestyle again quite quickly, to his surprise, as he fondly remembered his roots and enjoyed being back in his element.

He spent his days relaxing in the coffee houses, catching up with the men in the village, and sharing stories about what had happened to him. A tremendous amount of interest continued to develop around him, and people who knew him before came from other villages to see him. He became known as quite a storyteller. He shared stories about traveling to Venezuela by ship and the eventual challenges he experienced in Cuba, what he'd had to do to protect himself, and how he'd lived on a farm. The more he shared his adventures, the more his celebrity grew. As time went by, he found he was really enjoying himself, and he became deeply attached to his day-to-day life in the village.

In Venezuela, he'd been busy running his businesses, taking care of his family, and keeping up with his schedule, his six kids, and their needs as they grew older, but in the little village where he'd grown up, he had time to himself. Here, he had no responsibilities, and he enjoyed getting up in the morning, having coffee with the men, sharing stories, and days filled with relaxation and joyous occasions with family and friends. Ninety days passed so quickly, and he still had not made any arrangements to return home. He wrote my father a letter saying he would extend his visit for another ninety days.

My father wrote back saying he understood and told him to take his time and enjoy himself. He assured him that everything in Caracas was under control and business was moving right along.

So my grandfather stayed. He became used to napping under the almond trees and picking grapes off his grapevines, drinking milk from his cows, eating goat cheese from his goat, and fresh fruits and vegetables from the garden. In other words, he learned how to work the land again. All the food they grew and produced was so that the extended family could live on it, and he soon realized that this was where his roots were and where his heart and soul belonged.

The next ninety days passed, and he still had not

made any arrangements to return, so my father reached out to him and asked about his plans. Once again, my grandfather said, "I'm not ready to return. I need to extend my trip again." Intrigued that my grandfather wanted to stay longer, my father extended his father's visa.

My grandfather proceeded to buy more property and hired people to work it, and during this time, he also got reacquainted with my grandmother, which was a second honeymoon in and of itself. She urged him to stay, asking, "Why do you have to go back? Stay here."

No doubt she had a lot to do with him staying for so long after all the years with him gone, wondering if he was still alive. But she never wanted to give up her son and dreamed of the day that he would come back and, by some miracle, they would be reunited. Then why would he want to leave? She treated him like a king and was still in love with him, and the longer he stayed, the more his love for her started to return and continue to grow.

Nine months passed, and my father asked my grandfather, "What is going on?"

"You know what? I am not coming back," my grandfather replied.

"What do you mean?" my father asked.

"I take naps in the cool breeze under my almond trees—I drink fresh cow's milk, eat grapes off of my grapevines, and work my land by giving people an opportunity to work for which they are grateful. Your mother and I have gotten reacquainted, and I didn't realize how much I missed my family and relatives. I am not coming back," he announced.

"Never?" my father asked, surprised.

"No—I have no intention of returning anytime soon," he said.

My father wondered, *Now what?* And then he asked, "What do you want me to do with all these businesses? And what do I tell the family?"

"Sell the businesses—sell them all," was his response.

"Fine—but what should I tell the family?" my father asked, unsure of what to say.

"I don't know. Tell them what you want, but I'm not coming back right now," he replied.

"Okay," he said, and agreed to handle things as needed in Venezuela.

My father had to think about the situation and figure out what to do. He found a way to start selling the businesses privately, without bringing much attention to it.

As they were being sold, he said to Louisa, "Here is what is happening. My father got sick and had to have a kidney removed, and he cannot travel, so I am going back to see him."

"What about the businesses?" she asked with a surprised look.

"The businesses are being sold, and the house is paid for in full. You can do whatever you want," he said as he assured her that there was plenty of money in the bank to take care of her and the children. "I will be back soon, and I will keep in touch," he said.

Immediately, my father went back to Palestine, thinking there was no way my grandfather would never return to his wife and six kids in Venezuela. But it wasn't long after he got there that he realized that my grandfather was serious about his plans to stay with my grandmother. My father couldn't imagine what was going to happen. I am still amazed now, thinking about the situation. But my grandfather seemed to put everything behind him, and no one could convince him to do otherwise.

He wrote letters to stay in touch with Louisa and continued to maintain the "kidney story" for a few years as their relationship faded away. He never went back to her.

Coincidentally, in 1949, before my father went to Venezuela, he'd married and had a son. And then he left. He wound up doing the same thing my grandfather had done twenty-six years before, leaving a wife and eight-month-old son, Jad, behind. My father stayed in Venezuela for four years in all, but when he returned to Palestine, he was reunited with his wife and son, who was then four years old. Everything was great, it seemed, with his family. However, over the next four or five months, it became clear that they they had grown apart and the marriage was not going to work.

But my father loved his first wife and son so much that he dismissed his feelings and attempted at great lengths to make things work. At the same time, he felt that they needed to be in a different environment and decided to move the family to Al-Bireh.

Because of its location along the caravan route between Jerusalem and Nablus, Al-Bireh was as an economic crossroads between the north and south. He partnered with his best friend, Yosef Samara, from the police force, to buy a business called the Queens Café. It was built on the second floor of a movie cinema in the nearby town of Ramallah. What made the cafe unique was that it was one of the few places around where gambling, alcohol, and hookah smoking were allowed.

Dignitaries from all over the Middle East would come to the Queens Café to have dinner, gamble, and smoke. Hookah smoking originated in ancient Persia, Iran, and India hundreds of years ago, and became embedded in Middle Eastern and Asian cultures as a prominent part of social gatherings.

Queens Café 1955

My father's business thrived, and he enjoyed working with his best friend, but the situation with his wife, and the fact that their relationship just did not seem the same as before he left, began to weigh heavily on his mind. He blamed his absence all those years on the fact that the marriage was not going to work out. That was another reason he wanted to move away and have a fresh start, but that just did not seem to be enough.

After a year, the gnawing feeling that their relationship was not to last kept eating away at him. He finally decided to confront his wife with his feelings, and they agreed to go their separate ways. It was customary in those days for the woman in the relationship to return to her family home.

She packed up all her belongings, got in the car with their son, and he drove her to her family's home in the village and dropped her off.

At that time, it was common for a man's children to live with their father, so after he dropped his wife off, he took their son and brought him to his parents' house, telling them, "This is what happened—we grew apart."

Shocked, they said, "We didn't know anything was going on." His mother took Jad into another room, not wanting him to hear the conversation.

Saddened by what had taken place, he drove back to Al-Bireh, leaving Jad with my grandparents for weeks without returning, giving himself time to process what life had in store moving forward.

7

New Beginnings
1953-1956

After all the drama and the unknowns, my father was too conflicted to stay in his home village and felt compelled to disconnect himself from it. Psychologically, that affected my father because of his successful time in the police force, his ability to convince his father to come back to Palestine, and the successful business he'd established in Ramallah, earning him respect from the people in the village. Still, he was devastated and confused by what had happened. Those feelings stayed with him for years, probably until the end of his life.

One must understand that, in those days, divorce was very rare in the Palestinian Arab Muslim society, and there was just no way he could move on with life as it was. Although everyone in the village was unclear about what had happened, they knew his marriage was over. Soon thereafter, their divorce was finalized and they could both move on with their lives.

At that point, he returned to Ramallah to focus on

his business. He'd gone from having only a third-grade education to joining the police force, where he got an education and became an expert in sophisticated Arab speech, writing, and dialect, to becoming a radio news broadcaster. At first, broadcasting was a part-time gig while he was running the business, but he actually went to a studio to do the local news twice a day.

However, when my father was thirty-three years old, he started to think about the rest of his life, and starting a new family was top of mind. He'd noticed a young lady shopping with her mother when he and his partner took a break on their patio, which overlooked the hustle and bustle in the streets below. She was petite and had beautiful blonde hair and blue eyes, which was uncommon in a Palestinian woman. My father kept noticing her and was intrigued, but back then, a man could not simply walk up to a woman and speak to her without permission from her family.

My father said to his partner, Yosef, "I've noticed this young lady shopping with her mother across the street almost every other day. I wonder who she is and what family she comes from."

"Oh, I know her family," Yosef said.

Jamil Abedeljali, my mother's father, in 1965

"What do you mean?" my father asked.

"Her dad is Jamil Abedeljali. I know some of her brothers, too. She comes from a big family, and they live in Al-Bireh," he replied.

My father said, "I need to meet her father and the family."

That was the first step. If a man was interested in a woman, he had to meet with her father and family first. Even though my father was married before, he felt compelled to do things the traditional way.

Yosef contacted the family and arranged for my father to meet them. After a couple of visits, my father was convinced that Jamileh and her relationship with her family were right for him. Soon after that, he asked her father for her hand in marriage.

My grandfather acknowledged his request and assured him that the family would respond with next steps. Sure enough, my grandfather sent Ahmad, his oldest son, and his nephew, Hasan, to the restaurant to meet my father.

My grandfather told them, "I would like for you to go to his place of business to ensure that he is who he says he is. Find out if he is the owner of the restaurant and if he successful. I want to know if he will be able to take care of my daughter."

When the two young men arrived at the restaurant, my father had no clue who they were and greeted them as he did all his customers. He walked them to a nice table and ensured they received good service. They ordered something to drink and eat, and, afterward, reported back to my grandfather.

Ahmad said, "He is the real deal. He runs a hopping business and broadcasts the local news on the radio. When I asked him about his background, he told us he was married before, had a son, and served in the British Police Force as a mounted police officer."

"Okay," my grandfather replied, receiving the assurance he needed.

My father had no idea those men were there to find out information about him so that he could marry their sister, my mother. My grandfather invited him back to the house, and this time, he had a chance to see my mother up close and get to know more about her. When he was introduced to the brothers and cousins, he realized who those two men were who'd visited the restaurant.

Within a week, my father asked her father for her hand in marriage. My grandfather said yes—and then my father conferred with her and the rest of the family. He explained to her about his interest and request to marry her, and she agreed. Back then, there was no dating— it was the closest thing to an arranged marriage without it being an arranged marriage. In the early days of the Middle East, arranged marriages served as a way of creating alliances among families.

My father now had to tell his parents in Al-Mazra'a that he was getting remarried, so he made the visit by driving back to their home and told them the news. He hadn't seen them in months, and their response was, "What do you mean? You have to marry someone from our village."

He said, "No, that is not happening. I have found someone in Al-Bireh that I am going to marry. I already asked for her hand in marriage, and her family has agreed."

"No, this is not right," they said.

My father, who was thirty-three years old at the time, put his foot down and said, "Listen, this is who I am marrying. Either you accept that or not. You can be a part of it or not."

My grandmother gave in sooner and more smoothly than my grandfather, and started to convince him by saying, "We have to support him if this is what will make him happy after what he has already been through." Reluctantly, he didn't say anything and went along with the process.

It was then that a day and time would be arranged for a group of men made up of prominent people and relatives, including the head of the village, the Mukhtar (the mayor), to go and speak to her family on behalf of my father's family to ask for her hand in marriage officially. Two busloads of people from Al-Mazra'a went to the Tulba (which means "to request"), which took place outside a coffee shop just up the street from where my grandparents in Al-Bireh lived. Coming from a very humble family, my grandfather, Jamil, worked in a rock quarry, had eleven children, and didn't have much, but was very well respected in the community.

No women were there; it was all men from the villages, as per tradition, for asking for the hand in marriage of a young lady. If, later in life, there were any issues or problems with the arrangement of such a marriage, it would be up to these same men to gather together and help resolve those issues.

When they arrived at the coffee shop, Middle Eastern coffee was served to everyone, including my grandfather, Ali. At this point, he was still upset about the marriage because my father was not remarrying someone from the village. He was so upset that he threw that small cup and saucer into the street.

My father looked at him and thought he would start a scene, but a guy grabbed my grandfather's arm and asked, "What are you doing? You have to calm down."

He calmed down, but even as the Mukhtar started the event, my grandfather had a sour look on his face. He was not interested in any of it. The Mukhtar stood up and gave a long speech about who my father and mother were and why they were all there. He ensured the men from Al-Mazra'a they were welcome. After the rather long but eloquent speech regarding their presence, there were accolades toward the people of Al-Mazra'a.

When my grandfather heard those words, it was like a switch had gone off. He stood up, put his arms behind his back, and gave a speech that everyone in attendance would remember. He realized that they were great people and was in total acceptance of his son marrying into such a humble family who was so hospitable.

My father told me that he was so proud of how my grandfather handled himself and what he did, and that it resolved a lot of tension between them and turned their relationship around for the better. Now that the official part of the marriage completed, my father returned to my mother's home, where he had an opportunity to get to know his future bride. At twenty-five and the oldest of eleven children, she had spent most of her life taking care of her younger siblings, so she was happy and ready to get married. Besides, my father was a good-looking, prominent business owner and quite successful.

My parents' engagement picture, circa 1956

My parents with my grandfather after getting
married in September 1956

My father—circa 1958
(after my parents
married)

In September 1956, a week after the Tulba, my
parents were married on
two separate occasions;
one happened in the Al-
Mazra'a ash-Sharqiya,
and another party took
place in Al-Bireh.
Everyone was invited to
all the parties, which
lasted three days, so if
they missed a day, they
could always catch up
and enjoy the music,
delicious finger foods,
and socializing. After
their wedding celebra-

My older sister, Jehad, in 1959 with my
parents

tion, my parents moved into an apartment in Ramallah, and eventually, my two older sisters were born: Jehad in 1957, and Nehad in 1959.

After Nehad was born, my father made a strategic career decision—they had sold the business and decided it was better for him to return to South America because he had a sense of the business environment and opportunities after being there for four years and running my grandfather's businesses. He left my two older sisters and mother for another four years—from 1959 to 1963—and went back to Venezuela.

8

Back to Venezuela
1959-1963

He returned to Venezuela, but told no one he was coming, not even Louisa, whom my grandfather had left behind. However, he had kept in touch with her, and my grandfather never stopped writing to her nor did he forget about their children. Remember, she thought he couldn't travel due to health reasons, so in her mind, he didn't abandon their commitment and she had been financially secure after the sale of the businesses.

When my father arrived in Venezuela, Louisa and the children were surprised to see him, as they never thought they would see him again. Grateful he was back, Louisa welcomed him with open arms, and he set out restarting the clothing and fabric business my father had founded. My father always had a lot of business sense, however, this time he took a different approach than my grandfather and decided also to start helping people with what we today call micro businesses.

Knowing that many Middle Easterners coming to the

area, often with absolutely nothing, were interested in finding prosperity, he would set them up to be door-to-door salesmen, just like my grandfather had set out to be after leaving the farm. He took on three or four at a time and gave them each a suitcase full of merchandise, such as necessary clothing, general home necessities, such as irons, to sell.

Once the suitcase was empty, he'd tell them, "You will come back and pay me for selling the merchandise I gave you initially, and I will refill the suitcase again." This could be compared to a wholesale business, allowing new arrivals to profit. The people were grateful for the opportunity and appreciated him helping them succeed. It would take them about six months to a year before they would no longer need to borrow from him.

He ran his own business while caring for his siblings and Louisa. In 1961, while he was there, his sister, Sensione, the oldest of my grandfather's other six children, announced she was getting married. She had met her future husband while working, and my father had to ensure he came from a respectable family. They were married in a church, since most Venezuelans were Christian at that time, and all the children were raised as Christians while incorporating some traditional Middle Eastern ways of life. Sensione asked my father to walk her down the aisle on the day of her wedding, and he often spoke about that day fondly, grateful for the unique experience and being able to be a part of his sister's life journey.

When Middle Easterners and Muslims get married,

fathers usually escort the bride to the reception. Sometimes, they have completed the nuptials beforehand, and then the bride and groom are announced as they come into the reception area together. My father felt proud as he reported to my grandfather that Sensione had gotten married and that he had walked her down the aisle, ensured the wedding day

Sister Jehad circa 1960

was special, that the young man she married came from a fine family, and that she would be well taken care of.

While my father was in Venezuela, he helped his other younger siblings continue their education and made sure they had what they needed to go to school. The cost of living was minimal, and I remember him telling me he had left $15,000 in a Venezuelan bank when he first departed in 1953 to return to Palestine; we can only imagine what that would be worth today. He explained that his siblings were always at the forefront of his mind, and he spoke of them fondly. Part of him wanted to stay in Venezuela to make sure they were okay and provided for because of their obvious kinship, although once he left in 1963 to go back to Palestine, it was for good. He never returned to Venezuela, and they never visited Palestine. I am not sure how long communication went on, but he probably stayed in touch with them until 1967, when the Arab Israeli War broke out.

He sold everything in Venezuela and traveled by boat, taking with him a prized possession—a brand-new vehicle called a DeSoto. Undoubtedly, it cost a considerable amount to have it shipped, even back then, but in Palestine, cars were not plentiful. The fact that he was bringing back a new, American-made DeSoto to the Middle East made it clear that this unique automobile meant a lot to him. The DeSoto make was founded by Walter Chrysler on August 4, 1928, and introduced for the 1929 model year. The DeSoto logo featured a stylized

image of Spanish explorer Hernando de Soto. Many were attracted to the newly designed arched headlamps, vertical hood louvers, and great-looking interior.

9

Return to Palestine
1963-1968

Leaving Venezuela in 1963, my father returned to Palestine after four years, but he was fortunate to have been successful and experienced great prosperity. This prepared him to re-establish himself in Palestine after being gone from my mother and two sisters, who didn't really know him, since they were born in 1957 and 1959, respectively.

If you recall, my mother was living in an apartment in a nice part of Al-Bireh, and he would send money back to her, so they were in good financial condition and didn't need anything. The oldest of eleven children, my mother's six brothers and four sisters were a huge support system in the four years my father was gone, but that did not make it any easier. Being away for four years was challenging, especially since they hadn't been married for very long before he left.

When he returned, he began preparations for re-establishing himself by opening a new fabric and menswear business in Ramallah, in the same area where the Queens restaurant was located. His specialty was tailored clothing, and he became well-known in the custom clothing business. After all, no one in the area offered his type of service, and he brought a unique service to the area. Offering customized clothing meant everything, from the consumer choosing a fabric to make a dress or suit to tailoring suits and pants for men. He really enjoyed dressing nicely himself, always wearing a suit and tie daily throughout his life.

Now, he had to figure out where they would live, and, therefore, decided to build a house, which was a big deal back then. Of course, there was no such thing as financing or getting a bank loan, but he didn't want to build a house in the village of Al-Mazra'a. He wanted to live in Al-Bireh and be close to the business. He had plenty of property in Al-Mazra'a to build on, but he had an issue with everything that had happened with his first marriage and didn't want to build a house where all the drama had occurred. Plus, it was too far from his business, so he concluded that he would build in Al-Bireh. However, he was in a quandary because he couldn't find a piece of property to build on.

In Ramallah in 1964, after his return to Palestine

My maternal grandfather understood his predicament and said, "We have enough space next to our house." Back then, it was common for family members to build next to each other. My grandfather had enough property to allow my father to build a house next door, facing the main road.

"If you have the money to build a house, you can build right here," my grandfather said. Since my grandfather knew how to build homes, he immediately took a shovel and started digging the foundation. That is how serious he was about it; he truly was a special man.

The home-building process began, and my father built our home on my grandfather's property. To build a new house is one thing, but to have a three-bedroom, one-bath house with a full kitchen, living room, and dining room was a big deal in those days. Because of his fortunate time in Venezuela and successful businesses, not only did they build the house, but they also ordered furniture from Great Britain. That house also had a phone, which, in the mid-60s, was very uncommon. They even had a washer and dryer, something no one could afford back then. Plus, he had a brand-new white Desoto parked in the driveway. My father was a very advanced and progressive thinker who led a good life. Even though he didn't make much money in his days, we always lived well.

In 1964, my third sister, Kholoud, was born and his business flourished. Before the Arab Israeli War, freedom of passage to cross into any other area, such as Jordan, Syria, Lebanon, or Egypt, was possible, much like traveling from state to state in the United States. There were no custom stations to stop at, and he would travel to all those areas to order and buy merchandise to restock his business. Amman, Jordan's capital, was his central point of wholesale purchases, and he would travel there frequently.

As his business grew and time went on, I was born in August 1965, which was a big deal for my mother and father because I was the first boy in the family.

On one occasion in 1966, as he traveled to Amman to buy merchandise, he noticed a police officer behind him on a motorcycle. After driving down the road a little, the police officer turned on his lights to pull him over.

Me at one year old with parents in July of 1966

He pulled over, and when the officer approached him, he exited the car. They exchanged pleasantries, and my father asked, "What is the problem?"

"No, there is no problem at all. There is someone in the Jordanian Parliament who would like to meet you," the officer replied.

"Who would that be?" my father asked with a quizzical look on his face. When the officer told him the name, my father replied, "I don't know him."

"Well, he wants to introduce himself to you. If you follow me back to town, I will take you to him," the officer said kindly.

"Sure. Okay. I will follow you," my father answered. He had no issue with that. He got back in his car and drove behind the police officer to the Parliament building, where the officer took my father to an office. He said to the secretary at a desk, "This is the man he wants to meet."

Just then, the inner office door opened, and a man motioned to my father and said, "Yes, please come in."

My father, dressed in a suit and tie, walked in and quickly realized that this man was one of the top officials in the Jordanian Parliament. He was offered coffee, and they exchanged pleasantries until my father said, "I am confused—why am I here? Why did you want to meet me?".

The gentleman replied, "I want to buy your car."

My father, surprised by the request, respectfully said, "Well, it is not for sale."

"No? Everything is for sale," the gentleman replied.

"Yes, but I can't replace that car here. It's only three years old, and I brought it back from Venezuela. It is my prized possession, and I had to wait thirty days for it because it came by boat," my father said insistently.

"I understand all of that, and that is why I want to buy it," the gentleman said. "I respect what you went through and all your success. I understand this car means a lot to you, and I will make it worth your while. Whatever you paid for it, I will pay double that amount."

My father was not surprised by this offer, as the car received much attention in town. After all, it was an American-made car, and he was proud to own it. He was especially proud of the fact that an official of the Jordanian Parliament wanted it. My father thought that if he sold him that car, it would help him establish some crucial relationships, not only for him, but for his friends. His days as a police officer and broadcaster were important for him, as they brought him prestige, but he never considered that it would lead to any political relationships. He was not necessarily interested in politics, but it intrigued him to have that connection and have an opportunity to be associated with people in the Jordanian Parliament.

My father told him, "Let me go home and think about it, and I will let you know within a week."

"Yes, absolutely," the gentleman replied. "I look forward to hearing from you again soon."

My father went home and talked about it with my grandfather and mother, explaining that he could double the money he had paid for the vehicle when he purchased it.

"You have driven the car for three years—sell it," my grandfather said, who was also intrigued with this association, especially from a business growth standpoint, as they both had entrepreneurial minds.

My father returned to the man's office the following week and said, "I will sell my car to you."

Being a prominent man who wanted to drive a

unique vehicle, the man was thrilled and paid my father for the car. That was the beginning of a long-term relationship. My father became friendly with all the major players in the Jordanian Parliament and started getting into politics, where his communication skills from his broadcast days and his dapper appearance served him well.

My father started organizing events and dinner parties once or twice a week. My mother cooked for people from Parliament who would come to the house for dinner. Ultimately, my grandfather, Ali, got acquainted with them as well, and my father thought it would lead to an actual political position because he was so engaged in their activities and knowledge of world affairs related to the Middle Eastern conflicts and the Palestinian people. He was that way to the end of his life. As time went on and he got more involved in the goings-on, he heard about things that were not normally mainstream or discussed throughout the community.

He thought the next chapter of his life would involve being a business owner and holding a political position. He wrapped his head around that and learned more about what that life looked like. However, things were getting more intense with the Palestinians, and it was never peaceful after the establishment of the state of Israel.

The war in 1967 came as a result of years of increasing tension and vicious border skirmishes between Arabs and Israelis. The border between Egypt and Israel was relatively quiet. The biggest crisis was Israel's northern border with

Syria, where they fought over disputed territory and Syria's attempts to divert the river Jordan away from Israel's national water grid. The Syrians sheltered Palestinian guerrillas, who were mounting raids into Israel.

Western powers had no doubt which side in the Middle East was stronger on the eve of war in 1967. Israel was militarily unchallengeable by any combination of Arab states, at least during those next five years. The Israeli Air Force command, training, equipment, and services were more prepared for war than ever before. Well-trained, tough, and self-reliant, the Israeli soldier has a strong fighting spirit and would willingly go to war to defend his country. As you can imagine, the border wars stoked the tension, as Arab states had as much fighting spirit and determination in their plight against Israel.

Palestinian guerrillas broke through the border fence. Israel condemned them as terrorists; it believed that to deter and punish them, it had to hit back hard. A big Israeli raid into the Jordanian-occupied West Bank, targeting the village of Samua, in November 1966 followed a land mine attack inside Israel. The raid caused an uproar among Palestinians in the West Bank. Hussein was shocked. He told the US Central Intelligence Agency (CIA) that, for three years, he had been in secret talks with Israel; his Israeli contacts had sent him assurances there would be no reprisals on the morning of the raid.

Hussein imposed martial law on the West Bank and became more convinced than ever that his throne was in jeopardy and that angry Palestinians could overthrow him. He feared a coup by radical proponents of Nasser, who was the Egyptian president at the time.

The march to war continued, with escalating trouble on the Israel-Syrian border, as Israel was aggressively pushing its claims to disputed territory in the border area by cultivating fields in demilitarized areas with armored tractors.

It came to a head with a full-scale air and artillery battle between Israel and Syria on April 7, 1967. Then, an intervention by the Soviet Union changed everything. On May 13, Moscow delivered a warning to Cairo that Israel was massing troops on the border with Syria and would attack within a week. In 1967, neither Israel nor its Arab neighbors needed much encouragement. They plunged straight into the crisis that they had all expected for years.

Twenty-four hours after the Soviet warning, Egypt's supreme commander, Field Marshal Amer, put the army on full alert for war. More than half of the army, including some of its best troops, were bogged down in Yemen and in no condition to fight Israel. Amer reassured everyone that fighting was not part of the plan; it was just a "demonstration" in response to Israel's threats to Syria. Two days later, Egypt dug itself deeper into crisis. It expelled UN peacekeepers, who had patrolled the border with Israel since 1956, and moved troops into the Sinai Desert.

The mood was whipped up by Nasser's ubiquitous

radio station, Sawt al-Arab, the Voice of the Arabs. Broadcasting from Cairo to the rest of the Middle East was a vital tool of Nasser's foreign policy. Throughout the crisis, its chief announcer, Ahmed Said, read out a series of blood-curdling threats to Israel. The Israelis did not call Nasser's bluff when he threw out the UN peacekeepers and sent more troops into the Sinai, so he doubled the stakes. On May 22, he banned Israeli shipping from the Straits of Tiran, the entrance to the Gulf of Aqaba, effectively reimposing the blockade of the port of Eilat, which had been lifted in 1956.

After 1967, Yasser Arafat and his Fatah faction took matters into their own hands. In 1968, after several dozen Fatah hit-and-run raids occurred in just three months, the Israelis mounted a reprisal raid on the group's headquarters in the Karameh refugee camp in Jordan. The 1967 war made Israel an occupier, which is why, more than anything else, it mattered. The experience has been a disaster for Israelis and Palestinians. Israel built settlements for Jews in defiance of international law that says occupiers cannot settle their people on the land they capture. Israel, though, sees it differently.

My mother and me in 1968   **My father in 1968**

Things were getting intense with the Palestinians, and it was never peaceful after the occupation of Palestinian territory in the West Bank began. In fact, everything went to hell in a handbasket. My father's outlook on a future there deteriorated quickly as Israel occupied the West Bank where we lived—Palestinians, like us, lived under the rule of Jordan, but Jordanian law was thrown out the window. It was a short war that lasted only six days, and Arab countries retreated, surrendering the West Bank. The Sinai Desert of Egypt, Syria—and the Gaza Strip—were all occupied militarily by Israel. Everything shut down for two weeks, and no one could leave their home. The only communication about anything was through leaflets that were dropped by helicopters throughout towns and villages.

Grocery shopping was limited to a two-hour window, so we had to live on what we had until my mother could go shopping. If one owned a business, the owner could open it for a specific period of time, but they didn't want anyone to go outside. They would bus in Jewish people from Israel into Ramallah to shop at places of business with other customers, but the Palestinians didn't know what to expect.

Even though my father could open for business, there was no way to travel to replenish his supplies for approximately two months. They bought everything in his stores, but everyone was scared for their families. He told me he was left with absolutely nothing—every nook and cranny of his stores was empty. His two businesses were the size of a CVS store, so he had a lot of inventory. People bought everything in his store, and, as he put it, he was literally left with nothing but a needle and thread.

The interesting part about all this was that, although there was a war and the Israeli occupation was terrible, he said, "You know, the Jewish people are not the Israeli government." He established relationships with those Jewish people. One of the most interesting was an Israeli commander who brought his mother and wife to buy fabric from my father's store. As a result, my father became friendly with him. Even though he was in uniform, my father understood the political scope of things.

On one occasion, my father and two of his friends, including Yosef, had dinner at this commander's home. That was like sleeping with the enemy. It wasn't publicly known, except his friends thought it was intriguing. They had a cordial association, but the moral of the story was that my father was at risk for losing his business because he could not replenish his inventory. The Israelis didn't allow for free trade, and getting merchandise to stock in his store was impossible. The occupiers forced the Jewish clientele on him, and though the Jewish people themselves didn't take advantage of him, by the end of the day, my father knew that the Israeli strategy was to put Palestinians out of business so they would lose hope. At this point, he was forced to make a decision: either live with the occupation and operate his business under those circumstances, or leave, so he chose to leave and go to the United States.

10

Transitioning to America
1968-onward

My maternal grandparents came to America right before the war in 1966. About a year after the war started, my father realized we could not live under the occupation, as he was not free to prosper, grow his business, or care for his family at the level we had experienced previously, so in May 1968, he applied for a visa to the US, but it wasn't until early August of that same year that they were able to travel.

My youngest brother was a month old, and they left me and my four sisters with my paternal grandparents while they were gone. After three months, my father sent my mother back to Palestine with my little brother to get us ready to move to America, while my father stayed to

Me in 1970—First grade

secure a permanent work visa, which would allow him to get a green card and gain legal resident status for all of us.

The family portrait we sent to my father in 1968, when he was in America

My sisters were still in school, and I hadn't even turned four, so they agreed to let my sisters finish out the school year during the occupation. When my mother returned to Palestine to prepare us to leave for America, we took a family portrait to send to my father because it would be a few months before he would see us. We went to a professional photographer, who took pictures of my mother, sisters, my little brother, and me wearing a police uniform. My cousin received the police uniform as a gift from his own grandfather in America, and he loaned it to me. He let me wear the whole uniform, including the holster, but he wouldn't let me use the gun.

In June 1969, my father secured visas and legal resident status for my mother and all of us six kids. To this day, I remember all the preparations we went through to come to America, packing up what we could take with us and leaving behind what we didn't have room to take on the flights.

One of our first family photos in America, circa 1970

Our house was off the main road and had a sloped driveway. I recall two cars arriving to take us to the airport. I remember running down the driveway to greet them, as my grandfather yelled at me from the front patio to be careful so I wouldn't fall. We loaded up the cars and went to the airport to begin our long journey to America. Taking those flights was amazing to me as a young child—no doubt I was intrigued by how the plane took off. It was all new and exciting.

Part of our long journey included stopping in Amsterdam to change planes. From there, we flew to New York City. We were going through customs at LaGuardia, and I remember looking up to see a waiting area where people could look down on all of us arriving. My father and my uncle, one of my mother's brothers, were smiling down at us and waving. We had never been in an airport or been around so many people in our lives. It was fascinating to me and my siblings.

Me with Kholoud, Nahla, and Jehad
in 1971

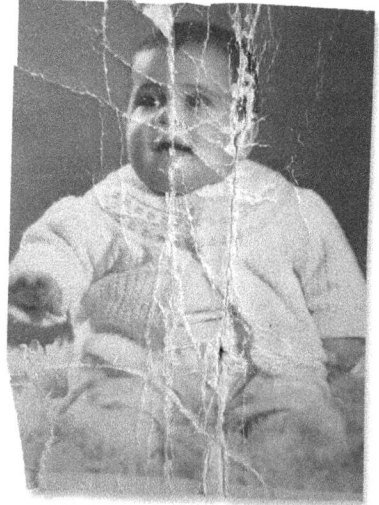

Brother Bashar 1968

After we went through customs, my father and uncle met us and loaded us into their two cars. My mother, two sisters, and my baby brother and I got in the car with my uncle, and my other two sisters got in the car with my father. He was one of the few immigrants who migrated to America from Palestine with money, so he didn't have to start from scratch. This was very rare, and one of the main reasons we got our visas so quickly.

My father had managed to purchase a yellow two-door Chevrolet Impala and had bought a small, white ranch-style house with three bedrooms and one bathroom on Route 7 in Virginia, near Tysons Corner. So we walked into a furnished home with a car in the driveway. What's more, he had bought a business with another uncle in Arlington, Virginia, a restaurant called the Barrister near the Arlington city courthouse.

It was at the Barrister that my father was convinced, after thirty years of smoking cigarettes, to never smoke again. One evening, a man named Frank, who was the chief of police and my father's friend. was having dinner at the restaurant with a group of people. He noticed that my father was a chain-smoking—and not only cigarettes. He smoked a pipe and cigars, too. Finally, Frank had seen enough. He confronted my father with the fact that he was killing himself. He blatantly asked my father, "Do you want to live a long time?"

With a confused look on his face, my father, known as Sam in the business world, said, "What do you mean, Frank?"

Frank said, "I have observed you chain-smoking anything you can get your hands on all night. You have to stop for your family's sake."

My father responded with, "What do you want me to do?"

"Hand me your pack of cigarettes, and hand me those cigars and pipe," Frank said. The pipe was silver with a brown bowl. Frank broke the pipe in half and crushed the cigarettes and cigars.

"I just paid five dollars for that pipe," my father said.

Frank replied, "Raise your right hand and swear to God, to your family, and to your friend Frank that you will never smoke again."

And just like that, my father never smoked again in his life. He told me if he took one puff of anything, he would start smoking as he did before.

Again, from day one of our arrival, we had a home, a steady source of income, a car, and a nineteen-inch black-and-white television. My favorite show to watch was *McHale's Navy*, something I looked forward to watching every day. I wasn't old enough to go to school yet, but I had a tricycle and a little peddle car, so my little brother and I were occupied at all times.

My father operated that restaurant with my uncle for two years and then sold his share of the restaurant to him and started his own restaurant in Frederick, Maryland. Although business with my uncle was good, the business in Frederick was challenging because the person who had sold it to him misrepresented it. It was more of a bar rather than a restaurant, and its clientele was shady. He thought he could handle the long hours, but after a year, he'd had enough. While we were still living in the house on Route 7, he sold that business and decided we needed a bigger house. He decided to take any job while he contemplated what to do next.

My parents at our first house in America in 1970

During that period, my father drove a school bus and learned to drive an eighteen-wheeler, which led him to work for a delivery company. While on that job, he had a mishap where he fell on the cement parking lot and badly hurt his knee. That injury prevented him from driving the truck and forced him to stay home on crutches while his knee healed. However, we still sold our house and bought a bigger house on Summerfield Road in Falls Church, Virginia. It was a two-story brick house with a basement and plenty of room.

I learned that, when I was born, my older brother, Jad, was sixteen. After we moved into the new home, Jad, who was in the Jordanian military, had a contentious relationship with my father. This was due to the fact that my father had divorced his mother, which caused Jad to become somewhat rebellious in his childhood. Even though my brother was known as the kid who always wore nice clothes, lived in a nice place, and had a father who was successful, he had a chip on his shoulder once life changed, and his parents were no longer together.

He and my father always had a strained relationship, and it didn't help the situation that Jad was a very intelligent and determined young man. My mother adored him to the day she passed away, but he was somewhat rebellious.

It wasn't long before my brother decided to join the Jordanian army, but he was only sixteen years old and was too young. He wrote a letter to the Jordanian commander and signed my father's name to it. The letter stated, "This is my son, who is eighteen years old, and I allow for him to join the army." The commander had no reason to believe what the letter said was not true, and, sure enough, Jad was accepted into the army in 1965. For six months, my father had no idea where he was or that he could pass for an adult at sixteen years of age. He did of course understand that Jad was very capable of taking care of himself.

Six months later, the commander happened to be in Ramallah and decided to visit my father at his store to catch up. When they started chatting over a cup of coffee, the commander said, "By the way, we are taking good care of your son."

My dad looked at him in shock and asked, "What? What did you say?"

"Your son, Jad," he replied.

"What are you talking about? We have not seen him for six months," my father insisted.

"No, he is in the army. I received a letter written by you giving us permission to enlist him in the army," the commander said.

"No, I did not—absolutely not," my father replied.

"We are going to yank his ass out," the commander declared.

"Wait," my father said. "You are telling me he is doing well? Following instructions, taking orders, learning to be a soldier, learning a trade?"

"Yes, he is doing great," the commander replied. "He is very intelligent and doing well."

Immediately, my father said, "Then you just leave him right there—don't worry about it."

Later on, when I asked Jad about his age when he joined the army, he said his age never came up. My brother stayed in the army, and as it turns out, if you are in the Jordanian army for two years and re-enlist, it becomes your career for a minimum of twenty years. In other words, either you are done after two years and leave or stay on, and it becomes your career.

When the two years were up for my brother, he was eighteen, and decided that this was his career, and, without giving it another thought, signed the necessary documents to stay on. Soon after Jad committed to staying in the army, the Six-Day War began between Israel and the Arab states. There, he saw bloodshed, fought against Israeli soldiers, and watched his friends die as the events of the war came to a quick conclusion.

Just before my father left to go to America in 1968, he went to Amman, where my brother was stationed, to visit him and check on his status. My father told him, "Look, I am going to America. Do you want to come?"

For that visit, my father stayed in the prestigious Palace Hotel, and that's where he and my brother had a chance to talk to each other as adults. It was then that Jad asked my father, "What happened between you and my mother?"

My father shed a tear, but he couldn't talk much other than to explain that they had grown apart and that it didn't work out. I always knew the divorce had affected my father more than anyone realized.

That was to be their last visit for a few years. My father left for America soon thereafter, and my brother stayed in the army.

My mother with me, my brother Bashar and my sister Nahla 1971

**My grandparents in
Palestine in 1972**

**My mother, me, and all
my siblings in 1972**

11

Falls Church
1971-Onward

Now living in Falls Church, Virginia, all my siblings and I had to make change schools. During the course of this transition, there was talk that we might move again to northern New Jersey, where we had relatives from Palestine who were in the clothing business. At this point, I was seven years old and in elementary school, and I was not aware that I had an older brother. We came to the States when I was four years old, and since I didn't know of him, there was never really any discussion about him.

About six months prior to the prospect of moving to New Jersey, my father received notice from my older brother, who was still overseas in the Jordanian Army, that he was done with being in the military. As you may recall, when you join the Jordanian Army, you are required to put in at least two years, and when that time is up, you either leave or stay twenty years.

My older brother had decided to stay and was now in his seventh year of serving in the military, but he had gone through many battles and had seen many friends killed in the 1967 war. No doubt, he had experienced quite a bit of trauma, not only in the war, but from the divorce, as he was quite young. After seven years of serving in the military, he contacted my dad and said, "I can't do this anymore."

So, my father, with all his connections in the Jordanian government, including the Jordanian Army and the commander who had told him that his son was in the military to begin with, went to work finding a way to get him out of the military and acquire a visa for him to come to America. Somehow, with all his connections and gifts given here and there, he was able to get him discharged

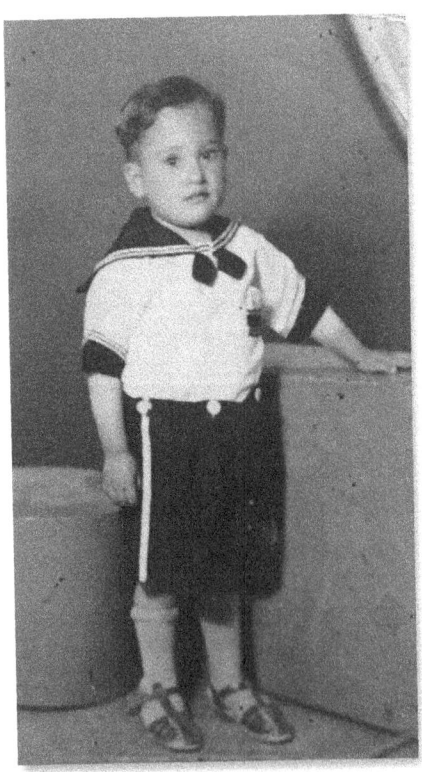

from the Jordanian military. Eventually, my father received word that Jad was getting out and coming to America on a tourist visa, but that was all he knew.

While my father was in New Jersey on a business trip, checking out the possibilities for opening a business there, my little brother, who was four years old, and I were sitting outside on our

Brother Jad in 1952

front porch early one Saturday morning. We were busy playing with some toys on the steps when, all of a sudden, a car pulled up that had a light on top. At first, we thought it was the police or some sort of military vehicle, but came to find out it was a taxi cab. A guy stepped out of the car, the trunk opened, and the driver lifted out a couple of suitcases, which he carried toward our house.

Immediately, I ran inside, yelling, "Mom—the police or someone is here!"

She came running out as my brother, Jad, who was tall and handsome, walked toward the front door, wearing a suit and tie and carrying two suitcases, and my little brother and I stared up at this guy, wondering who he was. At twenty-three years old, he was so much older than us.

As soon as my mom looked up at him, she exclaimed, "Oh my goodness, it is you!" and attacked him with a big hug. "We didn't know you were coming. When did you arrive in America?"

He hugged her back and said, "It's a long story. I thought I would just surprise you," as they walked into the house.

We all went inside as he brought in his bags and sat on the living room couch. My mom and he were deep in conversation about how he got there, but my little brother and I had no idea who he was. All of a sudden, she realized that he had nothing to drink and announced, "I need to make you a cup of coffee," and headed for the kitchen. My brother and I stared at each other and the stranger and started chatting a little bit, but I'd had enough, so I followed my mom into the kitchen.

While she was making coffee, I asked her, "What is going on? Who is that guy?"

She looked at me with an odd look and asked, "What do you mean? How do you not know who that is? That is your brother."

"My brother?" I asked. "What are you talking about?"

"That is your older brother," she repeated.

"The only brother I know is the one I was sitting next to on the couch," I insisted.

"No—this is your older brother, who was in the military and came to be with us," she explained.

"Wow," I said, stunned.

I walked back into the living room with a new attitude toward this man. Sitting down next to him, I looked up in awe and was so proud to have an older brother who was in great shape and looking so impressive, standing five foot eleven in his suit and tie. This was early in the morning, and my sisters, who were asleep upstairs, heard the commotion and came running down to see what was going on.

Immediately, my two older sisters knew who he was and ran up to him to give him a big hug. My two younger sisters were as confused as I was and asked, "Who is this guy?" as they watched my older sisters hugging him. The only person missing in this family reunion was my father, who was still in New Jersey, but he was supposed to be back the next day.

When he called later that day, we all agreed not to tell him and let him be surprised when he got home, especially since my father had not seen Jad in four years. The next day, when my father pulled into the driveway, Jad went into another room to hide while we all greeted him at the door. Since my dad had been gone a week, he was glad to be home.

My older sister said to him, "We received a telegram from Jad. He is out of the military and is going to visit our grandparents first, and then he will be here in the next few days."

"That is great news," my father said.

He sat down on the couch in the living room when my mother said, "There is one other thing we need to let you know."

"What is that?" he asked.

Right then, my brother walked out from the other room. My father looked up in shock as we watched their reunion take place. My younger siblings were still confused about the entire situation. Our happy reunion went on for a little while, but after a few days of letting him get settled in and getting reacquainted, my father asked him, "What are you going to do now? You are twenty-three years old—do you have a plan?"

Keep in mind that my father was very authoritative and hardcore after going through what he had experienced in life. His life journey had hardened him, and he was a no-nonsense kind of man. Though he was a loving, caring father who could be sociable, tell interesting stories that everyone enjoyed listening to, he was stubborn, believed in hard work and doing the right thing. He expected Jad to be at the top of his game—there was no room for nonsense.

Two more weeks went by, and again he asked, "What are you going to do? Do you want to go to school? College? Technical school? Car repair? HVAC since you have that background from the army."

My brother said, "No, I don't want to go to school. Maybe we can open a business."

My father replied, "I am still contemplating whether to open a restaurant or another business in New Jersey. Until that happens, you have to do something. Do you want me to get you a job? Do you want to learn the restaurant business?"

"Yes, that would be worth exploring," my older brother said.

My father went to a family friend who owned a pizza shop and got Jad a job there. Even though he started working and being productive, the relationship between him and my father was never on solid ground, and they would disagree on a variety of issues.

My father said to him, "At least you are doing something until we see where we are going to go." He also helped him get a car, so he had a mode of transportation. Jad often worked late, but after a couple of months, he would stay out later instead of coming straight home after work.

My father thought that lifestyle was not good for

him and finally said to him, "I realize you are twenty-three years old, but you are coming home at two or three in the morning, and that leaves us concerned for your safety. You have to be home by midnight."

Jad decided he wanted to live on his own and moved out, leaving without any notice while we were all asleep. I only wish we had known—we would never have allowed him to go.

What we didn't think about at the time was that my brother was around young men his age when he was in the military, and he was doing what military men do when they are off-duty or not in combat. Whether it was gambling, drinking, or meeting young ladies, that behavior carried over, especially when he was introduced to the freedom of living in the United States. My father was attempting to protect him from going down that rabbit hole and said, "You can have fun—but you have to be accountable."

After another couple of months, my father still didn't seem to be getting through to him. I recall one stormy night I couldn't sleep with all the thunder going on. Since I shared a room with Jad, I noticed that he wasn't home yet, which was not unusual. But as it started pouring rain and lightning, my father decided to wait up for Jad to come home. He'd had enough, so he waited on the couch, watching television until my brother arrived home at around 3 a.m.

When Jad walked in the door, my father looked him in the eye and said, "Didn't I tell you to be respectful of this home and set a good example for your brothers and sisters?"

My father figured that maybe he was up to no good, but Jad did not see it that way.

They got into an argument, and my brother said something like, "If you would hurry up and make a decision about opening a business, then maybe this would not be the case."

My father was not the type you could say something like that to without causing some sort of confrontation. "I tell you what. Go upstairs, pack your stuff, and get out of this house," my father said, pointing to the staircase.

My brother, who was just as hard-headed as him, said, "Damn right, I will."

Jad went upstairs, packed his two suitcases, and left in the pouring rain while we were all asleep.

When I woke up the next morning, the sun was shining through the windows, and I looked over at my brother's bed, and it was clear that it hadn't been slept in. I ran downstairs and found my parents sitting at the kitchen table having a cup of coffee.

I asked them, "Where is Jad?"

"He left and he is going to live on his own for a while," my dad said.

"What?" I asked in disbelief, knowing for sure how stubborn they both were.

"He made a decision to be on his own," my dad replied as he took another sip of coffee.

Although I thought Jad would return later that day, we didn't see him for at least six months.

One day, while I was playing outside with my older sister and younger brother, kicking a soccer ball, a white Bonneville convertible with a red interior and the roof down passed by us on the street. The driver beeped and honked, but didn't slow down. We soon realized it was Jad, but he didn't stop.

We were all in awe of having an older brother and wanted him to live with us. I don't believe any of my other siblings understood the full scope of their brother and dad's relationship at the time, and they were too young to ask any questions.

As we watched the car go by, my sister, Nehad, who was thirteen years old at the time, said, "He must be living nearby." A tomboy and a rebel of sorts, somehow, she found out where he was working and called him. It turned out he was living two streets over from where we lived.

One night, when we were getting ready for bed, she came to my room and said, "I found out where Jad lives."

"Really? How?" I asked.

"I called him at work, and he told me where he lived. Do you want to go see him?" she asked.

"Yes, tomorrow," I said.

"No, right now," she insisted.

"Are you kidding? It's the middle of the night," I insisted.

"We have to wait for our parents to go to sleep," she said.

"Okay. Let me know when we are leaving," I replied.

In order to get to his street, we had to walk about half a mile through a heavily wooded area. When we turned up the road, we discovered he was renting a room in a boardinghouse. We walked through the front door, up the steps, and knocked on his door.

When he opened it, he was shocked to see us standing there.

"What are you doing here? Are you crazy?" he asked, concerned for our safety.

He still didn't want to tell us what happened that night when he'd argued with our father.

We asked him, "After you left, what did you do?"

"I walked a mile and a half in the pouring rain until I found a pay phone so I could call someone I knew who could pick me up," he admitted. It is funny to think that he used a pay phone, but this was 1972. "I kept working and was able to rent this room."

"OK, we had to see you. What are we going to do?" my sister asked.

"Look, I don't think Dad wants me to come around right now," he replied.

"Come around when he is not home," she suggested as we walked toward the door. "We have to go."

We all loved and cared for our big brother very much.

We had to sneak back home, which took us about half an hour, but we made it safe and sound and without anyone knowing.

Shortly thereafter, my mother's brother, my uncle,

called from Knoxville, Tennessee, where he had a business near the university, and told my dad, "There is a convenience store near the university that is for sale; are you interested?"

"I don't know," my dad replied. "I was thinking about doing something in New Jersey and have never thought about living in Tennessee, but I will come check it out."

My dad drove to Tennessee to look into the business and was gone for about a week. It was during that time that my brother came around to see us. My mom adored him, so she would cook him breakfast, and he would come by for dinner on some occasions, but like any concerned mother, she always asked if he needed anything.

One day, about a week later, when Jad was over, my dad called and said to my mom, "You know what? We are going to do this."

"You like it that much?" my mom asked with surprise.

"Knoxville is a really nice town, and your brother is here—you will love it," he said.

"Okay," she said hesitantly, knowing we were about to move again.

He came home, got himself settled, and bought that business. You can imagine the preparation of moving from Falls Church, Virginia, to Knoxville, Tennessee, and going through the process of selling the house. As my mom prepared for the move, she finally told my dad that Jad had been coming around when he was not here.

He was upset at first, but then he said, "That is fine."

My mom said, "Why don't you ask him to come with us, so he can help us, and we can put this stuff behind us?"

She always loved Jad and wanted them to get along.

"Okay," my father said. "Call me the next time he is at the house."

The next time Jad came by, my mom told him about our plans to move and asked, "What do you think? He bought a new business, and he will need some help."

My brother said, "Well, if he asks me to come…"

Immediately, my mom went to call my father and said to him, "Jad is here."

She handed Jad the phone, and my dad said to him, "Here is the deal. I bought the business, and it is a good-sized store or market with a meat business. It is about the size of four 7-Elevens. You can come out here—you will love this town, but tie your bootstraps on tight and get ready to work."

"Okay, I will do it," Jad said.

My father said, "I will be back in a week."

The day we moved happened to be Super Bowl Sunday in January 1973. I had not become a die-hard maniac Redskins fan yet, but that day, the Redskins were playing the Miami Dolphins. If that were happening today, I would have said, "You go ahead. I'll meet you there."

My brother was there to help us load up a truck, our lime-green station wagon, and my brother's car, and we moved to Knoxville, Tennessee. My father rented a beautiful house in the woods on three or four acres of land. It was a spacious home; the front part of the house faced the woods and it had a circular driveway, while the backyard faced the road, but there was plenty of room.

My brother and I only shared a bedroom for a few weeks before he decided he preferred the restaurant business and did not want to work in the convenience store business under my father's instruction. He and my father started butting heads again, and my father asked, "Why don't you get a job?"

"I don't know where to go," Jad replied.

"There is a tire factory in Knoxville, and they pay a lot of money to manufacture tires," my dad said.

My brother didn't answer him immediately, but finally said, "I don't want to work in a tire factory. I will go back to Virginia and work at a restaurant." My father agreed.

The room I shared with Jad had an outside door near the garage, and, one night, my brother got up and started packing up his stuff. He didn't realize I was awake as I watched him gather up his suitcases and walk out the door to drive back to Virginia. That was the last time I saw my brother for three years. He stayed in touch with my sisters and mother, but we physically didn't see him for three years. My father didn't blink an eye and said, "He is gone, like when he went to the army. So be it."

He fully understood that Jad was a man of his own and was capable of doing many things.

Life went on, and my dad carried on with the business.

12

Time in Tennessee
1973-74

After about six months in Tennessee, with my father running his business and all of us kids in school, the unexpected happened. My grandmother, with whom my father had always stayed in touch, called from Palestine. It was the fall of 1974, and he knew his parents didn't have a phone at home, which meant she'd had to go to city hall to call, which, of course, made him believe that something had happened.

My mother answered the phone, and after some pleasantries, she gave the phone to my father. My grandmother said, "Your father is not doing well; he was out working in the fields and came home one day saying he didn't feel good and wanted to lie down. It has been a couple of days, and he hasn't gotten out of bed."

My father had not been back to Palestine since 1968, so it had been six years since he had seen them.

She went on to say, "You need to come home and

see him, as his condition is worsening."

My father had just obtained his American citizenship, but he didn't have a passport yet. However, the process wasn't the same as it is today. Since he had lived in the United States for five years and worked and paid taxes, getting an expedited passport only took a couple of weeks. He could have come and gone with a green card, but it was much easier to travel with a passport.

I was about nine years old at the time and barely remembered my grandfather. My father prepared himself to leave, and as kids, it was explained to us that my grandfather wasn't doing well, and it was up to my father to return to Palestine and take care of him.

Unfortunately, as soon as my father arrived, he discovered that my grandfather had passed away the day before, so he was distraught that he didn't get there in time. Instead of our relatives from Palestine calling to share the news before my dad left, knowing he would be traveling, they thought it would be best for him to find out when he arrived.

Middle Eastern and Muslim religions believe in an afterlife and that once an individual's soul is freed from the physical body, they await a reckoning where they can account for their actions in this life. As part of this belief, Muslim funerals and burials are usually held within twenty-four hours after death, in order to free the soul from the body. In most cases, family and friends will accompany the funeral procession to the grave; condolences and assistance are usually offered at that time. Excessive or demonstrative mourning is forbidden, and condolences are brief. Friends and relatives visit the immediate family for three days to give their condolences.

My grandfather was buried on a nearby piece of property they owned. My father wondered who'd made that decision, and asked why he wasn't buried in the town cemetery. He was told that it was his uncle, who presided over him as a child, who'd made the decision.

When asked about it, he said, "I decided to put him there because it is close to the houses where we live, and we had to find a burial site quickly."

As far as my father was concerned, he couldn't prove any ill intention on his uncle's part; however, when he and I visited Palestine in 1985, he thought about moving him and asked the village Imam if there was anything wrong with relocating the body. It was explained to him that the body was buried in a shroud, not a coffin, with concrete all around it. He said that if he were to uncover him, all he would be moving is a shroud full of bones, so he decided against it.

My father explained to us that he was so disappointed that he missed saying goodbye to our grandfather, especially since it had been six years since he had seen him. Even though he was seventy-four years old, his death was totally unexpected. It turned out that he'd had a strangulated hernia from working in the fields, something that was hard to diagnose back then. As far as his family was concerned, he was just experiencing stomach pains. However, a strangulated hernia occurs when the blood supply to the herniated tissue has been cut off. This strangulated tissue can release toxins and bacteria into the bloodstream, which can lead to sepsis or death. Certain types of hernias can become strangulated and are considered a medical emergency.

The day my father received the call from my grandmother she explained to him that his father had come home with pain one day, and it turned out that his intestines were strangulated. He survived for a little while, but it got bad, and he developed a serious infection. When the blood gets poisoned, if you don't do something about it within six or eight hours, it can be fatal. Oddly enough, my mother passed away in 2009 due to hernia complications as well. When it happened to my mother, she was diagnosed with a small hernia in her upper abdomen, and we were always advised that she should be careful, as they did not want to risk surgery or put her under anesthesia at seventy-seven years old. We believed that she must have done something strenuous to cause the hernia to become inflamed.

It was 1974 when this happened to my grandfather in Palestine; the medical capabilities were twenty years behind what he would have experienced in the States. If my grandfather were living in the States, he could have been saved.

My father had planned to be in Palestine for thirty

days to spend time with my grandmother, but between the stress of his father passing before he arrived and traveling, he became sick with the flu and was bedridden. For three weeks, he couldn't get out of bed. My mother finally received a message about what was happening, and though it was not serious, she was worried about him, besides the fact that he couldn't spend his time on the trip as he had hoped.

When it was time for him to leave, he couldn't change his travel arrangements, and although he was still under the weather, he managed to get on the flight back to Tennessee. He had to get back to his business and all of us. He slept the whole trip back on the plane, and all he could keep down were liquids like soup and water. He had no appetite and couldn't eat solid foods. When he landed in New York, he still had to catch the connecting flight to Knoxville, Tennessee.

Amazingly, as soon as he walked off that plane in New York, he felt one hundred percent normal again, no more fever, chills, or upset stomach. Plus, he was hungry. It was like someone had flipped a switch, and by the time he was back in Tennessee, he was one hundred percent better.

Even my mother said, "Wait, are you okay?"

"Yes, I am fine," he assured her. "I got off that plane, and all of a sudden, nothing was wrong with me."

I am sure my grandmother prayed for him, but he thought it was a mystery.

"What changed? Why did you feel normal when you

got off that plane?" she asked.

"I have no idea," he said.

When he got back home, he decided to sell the business we were in. We had been in Tennessee for about a year, and when he received an offer, he accepted. We were on a new journey to leave Tennessee, and he started looking into Florida. My father had a strong entrepreneurial spirit and a sound business mind, and always wanted to be in control of his own business and not have to answer to anyone. He ended up buying a clothing business on the central East Coast of Florida in Cocoa Beach.

I always wondered what would have happened if my grandfather had lived a little longer, if my grandparents could have traveled to the States. It would have been so cool to have a relationship with them as a kid.

My grandmother passed away three years later. My father did not see her again until he went back in 1977, when she fell ill. Fortunately, he got there to help her medically with a blood transfusion, although at seventy-seven years old, it was more of a treatment, not a cure. I am not sure whether it was kidney-related or not, but the medical care over there, as I explained earlier, was not the same as it was in the States. It makes me wonder as well if she could have lived longer had she been here.

My father was not a very emotional man. The only time I saw my father cry was when my mother passed away in 2009, rather abruptly, due to a hernia. He was eighty-six, and she was seventy-seven years old. We flew back to be with him, and that first day we got there was the only time I saw my father emotional. He cried like a baby. Lots of the family were there, and it was such an unexpected and difficult time. My wife had a wonderful relationship with my mother and learned so much from her, and even today, her recipes, methods of cooking, and baking are a large part of my wife's meal preparation. Fortunately, for me and my children, many of the dishes she makes taste as if my mother had cooked them herself.

My mother's death hurt my father more than all the twists and turns he had experienced in his life, from not seeing his father for twenty-six years to having him pass away before he could see him, which I know affected him. But he was a strong man and was able to compartmentalize his thoughts and feelings. I knew he was hurting, and as he got older, there were times when I would find him by himself, deep in thought, wondering what his life might have been like. At the same time, he thought about all the adventures he had experienced and all that he had done, from being in the police force and going through that process, to finding his father after all those years.

Even when my grandmother passed away (as we had already left Florida and were now living in Rocky Mountain, North Carolina), I remember him coming home from that trip of her passing, and he didn't show much emotion. No doubt, he mourned his mother and father privately. It would not have shocked me that he had his moments, but we never saw it. As much as he was a tough guy, he was still caring and loving to us as kids.

When he fell ill (he was living with us at the time), my wife would walk into his room to check on him, and he would say things like, "My mother was just outside the window, and I was going over to talk to her, but by the time I got there, she was gone." He had dementia for about a year before he passed away.

It was always his mom who came to visit him, which happened three or four times. It makes sense that he would see her because she raised him, and his father wasn't around during his childhood years.

He was hard to read that way, being a man of his stature; the course of his life hardened him, especially growing up with his uncle the way he had. He didn't have a father figure, and his uncle was not the best role model. Going through the police force made him well-rounded, but it gave him some obsessive/compulsive (OCD) tendencies. Everything had to be just so, prim and proper. For example, he went to bed every night at a certain time and ate at a certain time, most likely due to the way he was conditioned as a young man in the police force. The whole thing shaped him, but even at five feet eight, he was larger than life when he walked into a room. I wish my son had gotten to know him, but I am grateful that my three oldest daughters remember him well, and my youngest daughter also has a recollection of him.

It is a weird dynamic when you put his whole story together and see his entrepreneurial spirit. Though he never became wealthy or amassed millions of dollars, we all knew it wasn't about that. We always lived in a nice house; he drove a nice car, like a Cadillac, and was seen more often in a suit and tie or wearing nice clothes and with shined shoes, but that was who he was. Dressing nicely was gratifying to him, and it defined him. As long as we were comfortable, we never wanted for much, and he felt proud for being able to do that. The fact is, my mother and all of us kids have all done well, and none of us ever had any issues. My older sister is a college graduate, my second oldest sister is a licensed cosmetologist, my third older sister is a nursing assistant and has been with the same doctor's office for twenty years.

I have my master's degree in business administration and have had a successful career as an automotive executive. My younger sister is also a college graduate, and my younger brother has had a successful career in the automotive industry. So, we never gave him a hard time and always did well in school. My mother always preached that, at the end of the day, it is all about the impact you have on people's lives and what type of children you raise.

Mom and Dad—1988

Father—circa 1984

Father and me—circa 1984

At my home in Palestine in 2008. This was one of the last photos ever taken with my mom and dad.

My oldest brother now lives in Jordan. He got married in the States and had three children. He divorced his first wife, his two boys grew up to be Marines, and his daughter works for the Department of Justice. They are all very successful and hardworking; I am very proud of what they have become.

Eventually, my brother married a young lady from Jordan and went back to live there and have four more kids—two boys and two girls. The girls are happily married, and the boys are in college; one is about to graduate to become a chemical engineer.

My parents waving goodbye to friends at their home in Palestine in 1999.

Epilogue

Words of Wisdom

My father went on to live until July 2011, when he was eighty-eight years old. We had lost my mother two years prior to that, but they had been married for fifty-three years. Even though he recovered almost ninety percent after having a minor stroke a couple of years before her death, we could tell his health was deteriorating. We had a close relationship, and it took a toll on me and my family to watch him continue to decline over the next couple of years.

I don't mind admitting that, after his death, I went into a depression that lasted quite a while, but I was able to get treatment. My father was larger than life to me, and I looked up to him in so many ways. His ability to socialize, especially with close-knit people, fascinated me, even though he was hard to get through to, and only a few people appealed to him. My siblings and I would often say he was out of his mind when he'd warn us about certain people, but as we got older and so much happened, I sat back and thought, *My father was right all along*. I also believe that my siblings feel the same way. He always had a gut feeling about people and certain situations.

Looking back at his life, from those years in the police force to working his way out of a life of poverty for himself and his mother, what they endured at the hard hand of an abusive uncle, and what he went through with his first wife, all of it had a psychological effect on him. It could be one reason why he was standoffish with certain people or found it difficult to associate with people he didn't know. However, he had an uncanny ability to figure out whether a person was good, a handy skill he taught me. Because he was so confident in what he was saying, he was very authoritative, something we wondered about on occasion, but looking back now, we realize he was right all along.

My mother was the opposite of him, a special lady who balanced him out with her very giving, loving, and trustworthy personality. One of my cousins described her as a beautiful Palestinian woman with blonde hair and blue eyes, with a "gleam in her eye," as if she knew something about life that the rest of us did not know. There was this wisdom about her relating to people, life, associations, and relationships. Known for being the biggest peacemaker on earth, she didn't like people in conflict, especially when spouses within the family had an issue.

My mother would ask all parties involved, "What went wrong?" if a problem arose in their relationship. She was passionate about understanding the full picture of what went on in any situation. She balanced my father out in that regard. As I previously mentioned, my father was not a very wealthy man; he was more interested in living a comfortable and happy life. We always lived in a nice house, he always drove a nice car, and he was always well-dressed. For both of my parents, it wasn't about being wealthy financially, but more about how one raises their children and lives their life.

As hard as it was to penetrate his personality or even understand him, he was very loving. I kissed my father goodnight throughout high school, and my siblings did, too. My father had a balance to him, no doubt about it, but at the same time, he was somewhat private and not boastful. No doubt, that was due to what he had gone through during his life, both personally and professionally. However, he didn't think everyone needed to know what was happening in our personal life.

Dad's last driver's license in America

I inherited that trait from him, too. Even though I am there for people, I am not an open book. One thing I noticed and learned from my father was that he was very organized, almost OCD, in how he conducted himself daily. He dressed to the nines, shaved every day until he couldn't, and his organization of personal items and clothing was bar none. Even now, my kids make fun of me because all my shirts are hung up in my closet, color-coordinated with suits, socks, and shoes laid out for the next day. He certainly had that effect on me because now I do the same.

From a business standpoint, my father taught me the meaning of hard work and often said the old cliché, "Money doesn't grow on trees. You must live to your means comfortably, but at the same time, you cannot sit back to wait for something to happen—you have to make it happen. You have to go after it." Those lessons help me professionally in many ways.

From the time he made me go to work with him at thirteen years of age in the summertime, when I would have much rather spent time with my buddies going to the pool or playing ball, it didn't matter. He would knock on my bedroom door early in the morning, so we could head to Amra's Men's Boutique to work. Every day, I had to put on dress slacks and a jacket, along with dress shoes, and go to work with him. As much as I despised it back then, when I look back on it now, it has helped shape who I am today, with a strong work ethic and good fortune. I was frustrated because he didn't pay me, and when I mentioned that my buddies sometimes worked with their families and received a paycheck, he said, "I pay you every day."

"What do you mean?" I asked with a frown.

"Do you pay anything for the roof over your head?" he asked.

"No," I replied.

"School clothes?" he asked.

"No," I said.

"Food?" he asked.

"No," I replied, realizing I would not be receiving any paycheck.

Of course, if I went bowling or to the movies, he would make sure I was cared for and he'd give me money. It was an interesting lesson, and he made me understand that there is more to life than money or the actual dollar in your pocket. There is so much in life that has to be taken care of, and it was as if he operated his personal life as a business. He believed in budgeting and saving; I certainly got that from him.

If one was a friend to my father, there was nothing he wouldn't do for that person, but at the same time, it was hard for him to trust and let anyone into his inner circle; I am the same way.

I have always loved hearing and sharing stories, and so did he—that was his passion. He loved telling stories, especially when it involved his childhood or working with the British Police Force. I can still picture him sitting around at a party or function with ten to twelve men, the group listening intently to his stories; like a peacock with wings spread out in all its glory, indeed he was in his element and proud to tell of those adventures.

My mother was more religious than he was, but he was knowledgeable in all three major religions: Judaism, Christianity, and Islam. Though he was a spiritual guy within himself, he didn't express it, but she balanced him out with her religious beliefs by praying five times a day, fasting, and wearing the hijab. My mother was very loyal and wanted to be there for him, almost to a fault. It was an incredible dynamic to watch them go through life, as they dealt with the ups and downs, the good times and the bad times; he was always a man's man.

Some people think I am a hard-ass, and at times, that is how he came across until you could understand him. Then it was game on—he was a different person. It took him a while to trust anyone. I am the same way today, especially concerning my wife and children.

I will never be as tough or aggressive about things that he was adamant about—he was one of a kind. He was hardened because of how he had to live life, and my grandfather was the same way based on what he went through and the challenges he faced growing up in the Middle East, ending up in jail in Cuba, and starting from scratch. My father and grandfather broke the mold due to their experiences in life, and the same is true of my mother. They don't make ladies and gentlemen like that anymore.

My kids say I am demanding, but I want the best for them. My father was big on education and didn't have to discipline me too much because I usually did what I was told. Every time my son or daughters do poorly on a test at school, I make them write five hundred times, "I will study hard for the next exam." While that may sound harsh, it does sink in, and I have realized that my old man was right—he was not crazy after all. I wish he could have seen how my children have grown up, but I sense my parents around me every day, especially when I see my son. My three oldest daughters remember them vividly; my youngest daughter also has some fond memories of her grandparents.

On a side note, bagpipes are also often referred to as an instrument of war, and there is no doubt that they were used as a motivational tool for British troops and as a means of creating fear among the enemy, particularly during World Wars I and II. Throughout my father's time in the police force, the bagpipes were always playing, and for years until the end of his life, he always had a cassette tape or radio station on so he could hear the timeless music of the bagpipes. He passed away at eighty-eight years old listening to that special sound.

My son was two years old when my father passed. We brought my father back to the States when my mother passed. He thought it was just for a visit, but we wanted to keep him here long term because he was starting to lose his faculties, and we did not know how he could go on by himself without my mother. I did all I could to keep him in America, but it was a daily battle.

He kept saying, "I need to go back home." Whether he dreamed that someone had broken into the house or that our land needed to be cultivated or worked, I don't know. He would often say, "I want to die in my home over there, not here."

We finally let him go, and a year later, we visited after my son was born. It wasn't long after we arrived that we realized he had the beginnings of dementia, as he couldn't keep our kids' names straight. He had named my son, Jawhar, and actually engraved that name on the doorframe of the bedroom that he slept in. Over the years, he had never even mentioned to me that if I had a son, his name should be Jawhar, which means "rare jewel" or "beautiful object."

My son was eight months old when my father held him in his lap and kept calling him Jawhar. We were shocked because we had never heard that name, but that is what he called him from day one.

"Where is Jawhar?" he would ask.

We didn't argue or say that his name was Jamil. If I had known that was what he wanted, we would have considered it, but we'd named him Jamil.

My mother was born on December 20, close to the birth of Jesus, she would always say. Though she was a devout Muslim, she held Christianity in high regard. She was proud of the fact that she was born around the time of His birth.

When asked, "What is the one wish we could give you right now at the end of your life?"

She would say, "My son will have a boy." Since we had four girls, it would have been a dream come true to have a son to carry on our family name.

She passed away in January 2009, and when we came back from her funeral, I was scheduled to start a new job on February 1. Then, on a day I will never forget, my wife, who never calls me at work, called. I was in the middle of a meeting when my cell phone started ringing, and immediately, I saw it was my wife calling. I jumped up to leave the room to take her call, something I always do if my wife or kids call, and when I answered, she was crying.

"What is wrong?" I asked, concerned as I was thinking something happened to my father.

"I'm pregnant," she said.

Shocked by the news because she was thirty-seven years old and I was forty-four, and at that point, we didn't expect to have another child. I thought it was special that we had four daughters.

"Okay," I said, trying to reassure her. "Well, that is great."

Even though she was happy, she was crying because my mother had passed the month prior, and she wished that she could have been there to hear we were pregnant again.

It was May when we had an appointment with the doctor to have an ultrasound so we could find out the gender of the baby.

"I want to know if it is a boy or girl," my wife said to me.

"Okay, but don't get your hopes up too high," I said.

The appointment was on May 20, and when we went into the exam room, jokingly, I said to the doctor, "We have four girls; this has to be a boy."

The doctor turned the ultrasound machine on, and, instantly, we could tell it was a boy.

My wife started crying, looked at me, and said happily, "We are going to have a boy."

Later, the doctor informed us, "October 29 is your due date."

Her pregnancy proceeded normally until we went for a doctor's visit in her eighth month and discovered that the baby was in breach.

The doctor said, "We can turn him so you can have a natural birth."

"No, you are not turning him—we don't want anything to affect his well-being," my wife insisted.

"Okay, let's schedule a C-section," the doctor said.

Later that day, the doctor's office called to schedule a C-section on October 20, but it never occurred to us the chronological order of events:

We found out my wife was pregnant on the 20th
We discovered we were having a boy on the 20th
The C-section was scheduled on the 20th
And as far as we knew, my mother was born on December 20th

Talk about divine intervention. As noted earlier, my mother's name was Jamileh, so that is why we named our son Jamil. We are still amazed at how often the number 20 appears in our lives. When I went to Richmond to run dealerships, the zip code was 23294, which adds up to 20. When we arrived for a visit at the hotel, we checked into our room, which was 520. When I worked in Canada and lived in a condominium in the downtown area of Toronto, the condo number was 2020. Our address in West Chester, Pennsylvania, is 1010, which adds up to 20. There are many other examples where every time I turn around, I see 20.

Anyway, getting back to my father, who adored our daughters, my only wish is that he could have been around longer to spend more time with them and my son. My two oldest daughters are now married with children (four grandchildren), highly educated, and successful. Our third daughter is a prosecutor for the district attorney's office in West Chester, and our youngest daughter has finished her undergraduate degree and will be going to PA (physician assistant) school. Our son is a freshman in high school and thriving. That brings a lot of pride and joy to my wife and me.

The immediate family in your life is the most important. Whenever I share one of my father's life lesson quotes, I always credit him for that advice. To this day, I still hold my parents in my heart. Though their physical presence is gone, my love for them is real and will continue for the rest of my life. The teachings they gave and how they raised me have made me who I am today, and I carry

them in my heart and mind because of it.

My hope is that I had an equally profound effect on them and that I will always feel connected to them, as time and space are no barriers. Even though they are gone, I believe in honoring them by how I live, giving stability and direction to my children and grandchildren. I am grateful that before each of them passed away, we had no unfinished business—they knew how much I loved them,

Last picture of Father in 2009 and that is what matters most.

Memory Lane

Dad, me, and brother, Bashar in 1998

My mom and me in 2005

From left to right: Mom, my sister-in-law, Intisar, my wife, Insaf, and Dad in 2007

From left to right: Bashar, Kholoud, Nehad, Joe, Nahla, and Jehad in 2015

About the Author

Joe "Jawad" Amra is a devoted father and husband to his wife, Insaf, and their five children. With four beautiful girls, Sharihan, Sharin, Sharuk, and Shahira, and their incredible son, Jamil, he considers his family the most outstanding achievement of his life. Providing for them has been his greatest joy, and his family's well-being has always come first. Insaf and he raised their children to be highly educated, strong-willed, and independent; they couldn't be prouder.

Joe is passionate about sharing stories that date back to the year 1900—sharing tales of survival and determination of his father and grandfather with his family and friends, just as he learned of them through his father, who shared them with him and others. This book is his way of honoring their memory and allowing his children and grandchildren to always have a written point of reference to their family heritage and legacy. He has always seen traces of his father and grandfather's stubbornness, confidence, and mannerisms in his children, and he admits he has always had those same traits.

Outside of his family life, he is known as a strategic visionary leader; Joe is a dynamic, competitive automotive management professional with over thirty-three years of experience in the automotive industry. He began his sales career and was thrust into management roles after only eight months. Nine years into his career, he became the General Manager of one of the largest Chevrolet dealerships in the country.

Joe developed a passion for human resources and the development of individuals in all dealership departments. His ability to create successful TEAMS and establish community relations helped significantly increase revenue and profits. As his career grew, his utmost motivation was always to impact people's lives positively, personally, and professionally.

With broad-based experience in retail and wholesale automotive environments as an executive in the industry, Joe has managed operations garnering as high as $500 million in annual revenues. His vast experience with all domestic and import manufacturers gives him a broad understanding of various brand business models.

His proven success has earned many awards for the dealerships under his leadership, such as the Elite of Lexus, Toyota President's Award, and General Motors Mark of Excellence, among many other accolades.

Connect with Joe Amra

To book Joe to speak at your company, conference, retreat, meeting, or as a guest on your podcast:

Email: joeamra@aol.com

Let's connect on LinkedIn:
www.linkedin.com/in/joe-amra/

If you are a fan of this book, please tell others…

- Write about *My Father's Son* on your blog and social media channels.
- Feature Joe Amra on your podcast or radio/TV broadcast.
- Suggest this book to your friends, family, neighbors, coworkers, and company leadership team.
- Write an authentic, positive review on Amazon.com.
- Purchase additional copies for the adventurers in your life.